ADRIAN LESTER
AND
LOLITA
CHAKRABARTI

A Working Diary

ALSO AVAILABLE IN THE THEATRE MAKERS SERIES

ADRIAN LESTER AND LOLITA CHAKRABARTI

A Working Diary

methuen | drama

LONDON • NEW YORK • OXFORD • NEW DELHI • SYDNEY

METHUEN DRAMA
Bloomsbury Publishing Plc
50 Bedford Square, London, WC1B 3DP, UK
1385 Broadway, New York, NY 100018, USA

BLOOMSBURY, METHUEN DRAMA and the Methuen Drama logo are
trademarks of Bloomsbury Publishing Plc

First published in Great Britain 2020

Cover design: Charlotte Daniels
Cover image © The Masons

A catalogue record for this book is available from the British Library.

A catalog record for this book is available from the Library of Congress.

ISBN: PB: 978-1-3500-9277-8
       ePDF: 978-1-3500-9279-2
       eBook: 978-1-3500-9278-5

Series: Theatre Makers

Typeset by RefineCatch Limited, Bungay, Suffolk

To find out more about our authors and books, visit www.bloomsbury.com
and sign up for our newsletters.

For our parents,

Bidhan Kumar Chakrabarti, **Ruma Chakrabarti** and

Monica Elaine Harvey, with love.

INTRODUCTION

We took on the task of this diary with reluctance at first. Whenever individual practitioners who are couples are put together in the public eye it is often with the tag line of 'celebrity', an inside look at how that couple operates, a peek behind the scenes at their private life. It is this part of being in the public eye that we both instinctively shy away from. The diary was also a daunting amount of work to commit to for over a year when we both juggle so many projects simultaneously; it seemed foolish to add another one.

But keeping a track of what we have been doing for over a year has been a very good thing for us to do.

Our jobs are often confirmed at the last minute, forcing us to live our lives in the moment. We never have any idea where we will be or what we might be working on six months into the future. We could be in different countries, working in a variety of mediums. Writing about the many projects we are involved in has helped us understand how we work and the results we attain. Reading back over this last year has been a reminder that we work hardest between the jobs that we are paid to do.

We graduated from RADA thirty years ago and have been together since. The business has treated us both very differently but there have been certain universal truths. This profession is an absolute gift when it works and a burden when it doesn't. The problem is you never know what's coming next, so you can't plan anything. Our aim has been to stay solvent and move forward. We often speak of our place in the industry as if we were playing chess, moving in response to the counter-moves of the business. We haven't lost all of our pieces yet!

There is a lot that has been left out of this diary. We have focused mainly on our work and have left out a lot of our personal lives. We reveal so such of ourselves in our work that you have to draw the line somewhere. We have deliberately not talked about our responsibilities as parents to any great extent. As actors, the industry relies on your ability to be able to jump at any time in any part of the world. There is no consideration for family. The hours are long and you are often away from home for days, weeks, even months. No producer wants to hear about your kids in that context. You must seem able and free. Thankfully we both understand that and, between us, juggle things accordingly with the help of family and friends. A firm commitment to family inevitably places a strain on work and our priority has always been to make sure our daughters have stability in a world where we have none. Maintaining that stability runs underneath everything you will read here.

In short, this is a work diary full of projects we have chased and created; meetings that sometimes lead somewhere and sometimes do not; development and rehearsals; productions and dreaming.

Adrian Lester and Lolita Chakrabarti

ADRIAN LESTER AND LOLITA CHAKRABARTI: A WORKING DIARY

Friday 20 April 2018

Adrian Lolita and I are in between meetings in London and get together for lunch on Charlotte Street. It's a moment to focus and catch up on the status of her projects. Every few days we try to do this, to catch up fully and let each other know how work is moving along. We're each other's sounding board and take the opportunity to test ideas against each other whenever we can. It's especially helpful when things are at an early stage of development. The writing projects she has lined up look like they will keep her incredibly busy over the next few months. We can never be sure, though. Our livelihood is based on a complete stranger's opinion of us. It's an opinion that we can't really affect and so we have to constantly offer up ideas then wait and see.

I go along to a Taekwondo class in the evening. I've been training off and on now for over twenty years. It's nice to switch my mind off work and do something completely different. I find the training a much-needed antidote to the arbitrary nature of the acting profession. Each class is structured, reliable, repetitive and based purely on a system of merit. The group of people that come along are very friendly and always willing to work hard.

There has to be a lot of trust during class, as completing self-defence techniques with an opponent or partner requires you to put yourself in very vulnerable positions. You have to quite literally give your partner an arm or a leg, allowing them to manipulate it until they have the particular movement right. If you feel pain or are very uncomfortable, then they are executing it well. It's no place for a big ego and so it's always interesting watching those who come to take part in the class but find it very hard to drop their status. They want to practise on others but stiffen up when it's time for others to practise on them. In this situation, when I'm teaching, I never confront an ego directly. I'll take them away from their partner and allow them to practise on me instead. I'll share a joke or two during the training, maybe even asking them to stand to one side while I watch over someone else. Then, when it's my turn to practise on them, I slow things down and talk to them at every point as I do the technique. Those who are stiff or locked into their own status just need more reassurance during the class. I don't know their history, they are probably holding onto themselves for some reason. I can't pretend to know what that reason is, I just have to respect it.

It was a good class. A chance to leave thoughts of the industry behind and reset. As the Korean and club flags are taken down and we clear away our things, my mind begins drifting back to work and the workshop I have to lead tomorrow. It's for the London Philharmonic Orchestra Junior Artists programme. I've prepared something quite technical for them because they are already so proficient I need to add to their high level of expertise.

Lolita   I meet Adrian for lunch. It's the good bit of the day, a touchstone point to re-examine where we are and what we want. I head off for an audition for a guest role in a new television series.

The part is okay – a few good scenes with a bit of a story arc and character. I now analyse every script I read, not just from a character point of view, but as a writer. It can be difficult because I see the function a character is fulfilling and often, the parts I go for, have more function than personality. So in the audition, when they ask me 'what did you think of the character?', I have to really try to think of something to say.

Anyway, the audition is fine. Vague. I used to feel like I could tell if I got the job because there would be a warmth in the room from the connection made between you, the director or producer and the script. But now, very often you get put on tape and no direct contact is made. So who knows? You audition and hope.

Saturday 21 April

Adrian   Still aching gently from last night's Taekwondo class, I go along to meet with eight members of the London Philharmonic Orchestra Junior Artists.

The workshop organizers, Isabella Kernot and Emily Moss, had written to me saying that:

> . . . we find some musicians are supremely confident in their 'playing' role, but far less confident in spoken or written communication off stage. There are also nuances to consider around manner in a rehearsal tea break, versus talking to a conductor etc. Not everyone realizes that in UK orchestras we also have the 'trial' system – if you

are successful in an audition, you are then invited to go 'on trial', where you are offered to work with the orchestra on various concerts, to assess how you fit in musically, and also socially (how do people get on with you when they're exhausted on tour/in the pub etc). This is where a whole range of different social skills come into play, that aren't necessarily taught in conservatoire . . . general health and well being/looking after yourself as an artist – [it would be] valuable to include and give a context to considering 'non-musical' aspects of performance . . .

The information and links they sent me beforehand allowed me to watch some of the people taking the workshop as they performed on TV's *Young Musician of the Year* runners-up and finals. I was a little blown away by the talent of some very fine musicians who at this point in their lives were wondering whether or not they would pursue a career in classical music. I think Isabella and Emily were aware that, although talented players come from all over the country and have very different cultural backgrounds, the people making their way into the renowned orchestras did not really reflect this.

My understanding is that a gifted musician would be allowed to play with an orchestra as an apprentice but may end up staying in that apprenticeship role for well over a year, sitting beside the more senior players through many concerts and recitals. Although apprentices play, they are junior to everyone else so are often the ones who make tea or coffee, watch over instruments on breaks, hoping one day to become a permanent player, perhaps reaching the grand height of soloist. Some musicians will sit in the same place, squeezed in next to the same people in the same orchestra, for thirty or forty years.

Getting along with your fellow players is essential. Especially at the beginning when the head of the section can decide if you eventually get the job.

It's incredibly logical that this should be the case, but I hadn't really thought about it until I had to work out what would be good for each of these young people in a workshop situation.

I decided to work on status with them. It's a very useful exercise that opens students up to examining patterns of behaviour that denote a person's status in any situation – the status you are given and the status that you allow yourself to have.

The exercise is something I learned from Brigid Panet, a great teacher/director, whom I worked with on my second job out of drama school.

I take a pack of playing cards, removing the picture cards and aces, so that I'm left with the cards numbered two to ten. With two being the lowest and ten the highest, I slowly demonstrate how the shape of a person's body and the sound of their voice changes as they feel an increase in their status. This exercise shows how subconscious body language gives off signals that are subconsciously read and accepted, but during this exercise we make the mannerisms consciously, bringing the signals clearly into the spotlight in order to look at their patterns and the effect they have. It's always at this point that the people taking the workshop begin to be aware of how they are standing, how they move and how they speak to one another. It makes everyone very self-conscious at first but then increases confidence in the room as we all play with the meanings these mannerisms give off.

After that I move on to Alexander Technique. It's a method of freeing the body from excess tension while carrying out everyday activities. Simple physical tasks such as standing and sitting are examined in detail and each student was shown that non-useful tension can trap your voice, strain your back and in many cases cause headaches. I want them to connect their breath to movement so they can carry out tasks with the least amount of strain and wasted energy.

My aim was to increase their confidence and social awareness as they think about a career in music . To get them to think about honest communication of feeling through the layers of insecurities, tensions and coping mechanisms that surround human beings. I may have been a bit too technical in my approach – I often am – but all in all it seemed to go well.

Came home and cooked a chicken dinner for when the kids got in from school, then got my gardening gloves on to move the remnants of a large dismantled shed from the back to the front garden ready to be picked up in the morning. Spent an hour moving rain-soaked piles of sodden wood with rusted nails sticking out of it.

All that chat about using breath, Alexander Technique and balancing strain. Time for me to put my money where my mouth is. . . .

Monday 23 April

Lolita   Last year I was asked if I would adapt Yann Martel's Booker Prize-winning novel, *Life of Pi*, for the stage. I loved the book when it came out and jumped at the opportunity. I have now written an initial draft and today is the first day of our first workshop on the script.

Having finished performing in *Fanny and Alexander* at the Old Vic a week ago, I have to put my other hat on. Although acting and writing definitely cross over, there is a clear shift of responsibility between the two roles. As an actress I am part of the whole, but as a writer I *make* the whole. So I am a little nervous – excited and worried: am I able to deliver what I think I can? This workshop is the first foray into testing the structure, characters and overall storytelling of my script. It's where my words get scrutinized and tested.

We're in the RSC rehearsal rooms in Clapham for the week. I've not been here before. Adrian and I used to live round here thirty-odd years ago when we were students at RADA. Needless to say it feels familiar but has changed a lot.

Max Webster, who directed *Fanny and Alexander*, is on board to direct *Pi*. Having worked with him as an actor, I have a strong idea of how he works to build character from the inside out and I also know how he can transform a fairly mundane scene into a theatrical feast. I am grateful to him, actually, because not everyone can accept me in both roles.

We are in a room with ten actors, three of whom are also skilled puppeteers. Simon Friend is producing: he joins us for the first read and then leaves us to it. I have worked with some of these actors before, and it is very satisfying to have friends in the room.

I am still amazed by the acting community. We work together intensely for days, weeks or months and then don't see each other for years, but when you do there is a familiarity and natural bond – we're still here. We're still playing.

The day goes well, I think. Hearing the script read out for the first time is less painful than I thought it would be. Often, when I hear my words for the first time, they seem gauche and awkward. But doing an adaptation I realize that although Yann Martel isn't here, I feel very supported by his narrative. This is his story realized by me.

The discussion with the actors about themes in the play is great. Talking of faith, truth, storytelling, fear, trauma, loss – life. There are many different perspectives in this room.

I ask that no one play his or her role with accents. There is a Japanese character, many Indian characters, a Canadian. I ask them to use their own British regional accents. Although in many cases accents add colour and context, I think it can also reduce the story. I have never heard British actors performing Ibsen or Chekhov use Norwegian or Russian accents. I have noticed that often accents are required for plays set in India or Africa. Why is that? If the cast looks like the parts they are playing, I don't need their accents to qualify their culture. I just want to watch people. In *Fanny and Alexander* at the Old Vic, there was no discussion that we should perform the play in Swedish accents. As we continue to rehearse *Life of Pi* without accents I find that, for me, it works, and raises the piece to a universal story rather than a cultural one.

After lunch, Max gets the actors to put the first couple of scenes on their feet. Everyone is very game to try the scenes in a myriad of ways – to play. I can see the scenes don't work but find it hard to articulate why.

I need to process all the questions that emerge and let the answers filter through. I am impatient and frustrated by the limitation of my words. I feel that many of the lines are flat and need a depth of history and character to them. Of course I hope that frustration is what will drive me to better writing.

I get home to the kids. Adrian is out at Taekwondo training tonight. The girls need to download their days. Am longing to download my own and process today's work, but that will have to wait.

Wednesday 25 April

Adrian   I have been asked to sit as a subject for some of the artists taking part in the Sky Portrait Artist of the Year competition. Up and out by 7.15 am, I'm feeling very tired and know I'll spend the day being stared at by artists and cameras. Only on arrival did I realize that it's the artists who are under the real scrutiny. Watching them cope with so much attention made me see how hard the task is for them.

Most of these artists don't spend their time being interviewed. They paint in private, giving themselves days or weeks to get their pictures right. Yet here they are having members of the public walk around and talk about their work literally behind their backs as they are trying to create it. On top of that, cameras are pushed around all day pointing at the artists, while they're painting or focused on me sitting.

I can't help notice how often the cameras and production assistants block the view of the artists to their subjects. Three artists are painting me: Rosso, TK and Emile. When the camera is pointed at Emile and his canvas, it stops him from seeing me. The runners surrounding the camera, chatting about what the next shot should be, block TK from seeing me too. Rosso, the third artist, would then try to carry on by peering at me over someone's shoulder. The painters took all this in their stride even though, at the same time, they were being monitored by the show's experts who frequently came round asking them questions about their work.

I am sat in a chair trying not to move for roughly four hours watching this go on. My mind drifts. Because I'm a geek, I start thinking about the observer effect, the theory that simply observing a situation or phenomenon changes that phenomenon. Which made me think that . . . 'The act of observing an act of creation, changes what is created.' Sounds quite deep, but in other words . . . 'God, I bet those cameras are putting them off.'

I suppose the idea, then, is to make sure they are all *equally* put off. In order to test their abilities as artists fairly.

A lot went through my mind as I sat there. The first twenty minutes were strange. Sitting and being stared at while doing or saying nothing, you feel incredibly vulnerable. I think that's because I'm only used to standing up in front of people when I've got some sort of character to hide behind. After a while, I began to go over an important script in my head. Camera operator and Director of Photography Luke Redgrave, whom I had worked with while shooting *Hustle* for the BBC and Kudos, had approached me a while ago with an idea. He had just bought the film rights to a novel by Michael Byrne called *Lottery Boy* that was just about to go on sale. The story follows a homeless boy called Bully as he tries to survive sleeping rough on the streets of London. One thing leads to another until the boy is chased across London by drug-dealing gangs and the police.

Luke asked me to write the film script and we've been working on it for over a year. I'm working on a new draft and had gotten stuck on some problems I had with the beginning. But, after a few hours of sitting in one position, hardly moving, I feel I have now managed to come up with a few solutions. In the car on the way home, I start writing. I know I've got to set down what I've worked out before I forget it.

Nitin Sawhney and Sophie Ellis-Bextor were being painted on the same day as me, both very down to earth and easy going. I chatted a little with Sophie about juggling parenting and this profession. It was good to meet Nitin, whose music has been played loudly in our house for years. I remember the first time I heard a beautiful track from his album *Broken Skin* called 'Immigrant', I listened while Lolita translated the Bengali in the song for me. One of our favourite Nitin Sawhney tracks is 'Sunset', the version on the album *Prophesy*. It gets us nodding our heads and singing through whatever task we have to do in the house. There are so many pieces of music that will stop me in my tracks and make me drift off into sing-a-longs. Maxwell's 'Ascension' always does that to us. It links Christmases and birthday parties with friends dropping silly harmonies throughout the song.

Anyway, after chatting to Nitin for a while I felt I was beginning to show my inner geek.

By the end of the day some phenomenal work had been done by all the artists. The portraits painted of me, Sophie and Nitin were excellent.

Lolita   The third day of the *Pi* workshop.

I hadn't realized just how much the workshop would rigorously test my material. The actors and Max are very nice, inventive and respectful as we pull my words apart trying to define what the drive of the story for each character is.

I had to leave early yesterday, for an acting audition, so they worked on the scene where the ship Tsimtsum sinks. They show it to me today. Ten actors creating calm, chaos, storm, distress, animals, people and landscape. They use everything in the room to tell the story – costume rails, hangers, tissue boxes – transforming them into fish and ship debris. One wrong step and it could feel like a Monty Python sketch, but they never put a foot wrong. Their intention is so clear that we see within it some beautiful, heartbreaking moments. It is exciting to see the possibilities.

I have crammed the story full of images from Yann's book but for the stage they need more time to establish themselves. I have an embarrassment of riches to choose from but I have to create a driving story within them.

These last couple of days I've felt quite daunted by the task ahead of me, but today I see how magical this could be and how fundamentally theatrical it is. In order to make this work, it feels like we have to create a new theatrical language for Pi and his world.

I love the perspectives in this room – different ways to look at the world, different cultures to inform our understanding.

I was offered a place in the writers' room on a new series for Sky TV today – which might be good practice.

I have also been approached about a very exciting multidisciplinary piece for Manchester International Festival (MIF) next year. This one really excites me – state-of-the-art design, dance, music and poetry.

My head is exploding a bit with *Pi*, so feel very lucky but slightly overwhelmed.

Half of my creative mind is always taken over by my role as a mother. My kids need structure and order, which seem in direct opposition to a freelance life. While I plan for what the kids need for the week ahead, I am also trying to keep my mind free to tell stories and play roles. Sometimes it feels like an impossible task.

Thursday 26 April

Adrian I have been cast in a new Starz series called *The Rook*. It's based on a book by Daniel O'Malley about secret government agencies that deal with people who have Extreme Variant Abilities (EVA): from precognition and telekinesis to photographic memories and augmented strength. The read-through is at the Bloomsbury Hotel. Once I arrive, I meet with members of the cast, the directors and the wider team of producers connected to Lionsgate and Starz. My role is that of an EVA, who is second in command of the British organization called The Chequy. The first two scripts are great, layered with character and plenty of action. That's normally all you get to read when you decide to commit yourself to a long-running story. You get scripts one and two and sign the contract in the hope that what follows will be equally as good. We all mill about greeting each other before sitting down to read.

TV readings are strange things. The actors don't necessarily give the text that extra oomph needed to get it off the page (the kind of energy you find in a read-through for a play). This was much more for TV performances. I found myself trying to stare at everyone reading so that I could see any choices being made for performance. Good bunch of people. Everyone seems to be pulling in the same direction. Should be an interesting project. Cycled home.

Friday 27 April

Lolita I woke up this morning with butterflies. It's the last day of the *Pi* workshop, ending with a short presentation to an invited audience.

I came home last night and rewrote one of the scenes. I thought I'd made some radical changes but when I reread it this morning they were minor – essential but minor.

I listen to the music from the musical *Hamilton* on my way into work. The lyrics remind me of the power of writing and what you can achieve if you stick to your guns.

We spend the morning rehearsing the new scene, whilst puppet master Finn Caldwell and the actor/puppeteers rehearse the tiger, Richard Parker. Finn and his partner Nick have made a prototype tiger. It has a great range of movement and gives us a strong indication of size and power – this is exciting stuff.

Adrian Morning meeting with Karyn Usher and Liza Zwerlig, the showrunners for *The Rook*. Chatted through the storylines for series one and shared thoughts on my character. He is someone who believes EVAs shouldn't be kept in the dark in any country but instead have their abilities celebrated. Keeping their abilities out of sight means they can be trafficked and used as weapons. My character is calculated and warm, but always keeps the truth hidden from plain sight. The audience shouldn't know whether or not they can trust him. The writers have placed so much messy human detail into the show it could run and run.

We talk about the mystery elements in the script. It's a thriller, so we'll be balancing the expectations of the audience with delivery. How do we prepare ourselves to keep very human stories running through what might first be looked upon as a genre piece? We have to keep the viewer intrigued, but not confused; they have to work things out feeling that nobody else caught it. These discussions are very important at the beginning of a project, and I get a great feel for the tone of the piece, as well as an understanding of how to pitch my performance. I come away from the meeting wishing I was more involved in its development. I'm itching to direct again and this would be the perfect project for me to do a few episodes. I'll raise that the next time I see Karyn, Liza and Stephen Garrett, our exec producer for the project in the UK.

I'm running a little late as I get back on my bike, making my way across London to the RSC rehearsal rooms in Clapham. Lolita has been working on *Life of Pi* all week and the actors and puppeteers are about to have a workshop presentation.

I arrive and see Katie, Lolita's literary agent, and lots of artistic directors present, some I recognize, some I don't. The whole thing starts with Max the director and a nervous Lolita talking a little about the project and what they've been experimenting with during the week. During the presentation the actors create a boat, a hospital, a scene in a zoo with animals milling about, fish in the sea and Pi's interaction with the tiger, Richard Parker. It gave us all a good sense of what might be possible with more rehearsal and more space. Creating scenes and characters using almost nothing in an empty space can feel a little like magic in theatre. It'll be really interesting to see where it might go, who bites. I hope things happen for this show.

Lolita   At 4.30 pm, about thirty or forty people turn up to see our presentation. My butterflies were well founded. There are several artistic directors of London and provincial theatres, literary people, producers, agents and friends. It is a full house.

I think the presentation went well, although I could hear a lot of gaps in my writing. That is always what happens though – the gap between what you think you've written and what you actually have. The response afterwards is positive. Let's see what happens.

I am glad when it is over.

Monday 30 April

Adrian   First day on set for *The Rook*. Feeling ill, nursing a tummy bug. It's quite a big crew gathered here on the South Bank overlooking the Thames. It's April and spring hasn't really made an effort yet. It's a scene where my character has to meet with an operative from a foreign organization to try and get information out of him. Every sentence is loaded with hidden questions and assumptions, so I'm standing in the cold, trying my best to look enigmatic in a suit while feeling a bit dizzy. It's raining a bit, but we carry on. Strange that even though the cameras are 4K ultraHD everyone is happy for you to keep shooting in the drizzle as they say the camera won't see it.

Lolita   It's my first day of what feels like a bit of freedom. It's been a busy year and today I don't need to be anywhere.

I take my time today – or I think I do.

I am curating an event as part of The One Voice season for the Old Vic Theatre in London. It is marking the seventieth birthday of the NHS. It will be a one-off event. I have called it *The Greatest Wealth*, after Virgil's quote 'the greatest wealth is health'. I have commissioned eight writers, myself included, to respond to one of the eight decades of the NHS in a monologue. Just to approach writers with an offer of a project, hear their ideas and facilitate work has been liberating.

My decade is 1980s but I was so busy coordinating the other writers I found my own ideas for the period elusive. Then I suddenly thought – I'll write about my dad. He's worked in the NHS for almost sixty years, working his way up from a junior doctor to an orthopaedic surgeon. It's an obvious way into the NHS for me, so I interviewed my dad a couple of times. Fact is so much more interesting than fiction but when you weave it together with a dramatic thrust it becomes something else. I enjoy interpreting facts, offering them up from an unusual perspective. It's what I did with *Red Velvet*.

I collate my workshop notes on *Pi*: there are a lot of them, a huge jumble of ideas that need to be put into some sort of order. Max wants simpler, longer, more engaging scenes. First, I restructure the story giving each scene a heading and story beat. Then I write all the character and story notes for each scene under their particular heading, creating what looks like a graph that charts what I need to do to the narrative and progression of each character. I stare at it all for a moment. I'll have to get into all of this later when I rewrite, but for now, I put it all away.

I will leave *Pi* for a month now, I know my thoughts will filter subconsciously while I turn my attention to working on the film of *Red Velvet*. I adapted my play about Ira Aldridge into a film script in 2014, when the play transferred to New York's St Ann's Warehouse and I've been working on it intermittently ever since. In my mind, *Red Velvet* was always meant to be a film but finding the right producers has been a challenge. I want it done well. It means too much to me to just sell the script. I've been trying to work on this draft since October but because of acting and other writing commitments have had to keep putting it down. It has felt like the *Red Velvet* folder in my head is always open and I've had to ignore it calling me. I cannot wait to get it done.

Anyway, *Pi* notes are done and now *Pi* is the folder that has to wait.

Speak to Katie Haines, my brilliant literary agent. The new project at MIF is looking good. I'm waiting for a meeting. It would really stretch my imagination. To collaborate with creatives from so many disciplines would be wonderful and it'll be a real challenge to set the narrative given all of their needs.

Wednesday 2 May

Lolita   I speak to writer Paul Unwin this morning on the phone about his monologue for *The Greatest Wealth* at the Old Vic.

Paul's piece is based in the 1950s and it's ambitious, sprawling and skilled. He is very experienced in writing and directing but open to feedback. He's a reminder to me that staying open to input can improve your work. I have some thoughts on his piece.

Collating this vision of the world by asking writers and actors who reflect inclusivity, feels therapeutic. I know the profession is changing at last but to be part of that change is empowering. For the past twenty-eight years I have often been the only person of colour in so many rooms and the fact that rarely happens now, is a relief.

I have a meeting at the Old Vic with producers Jessie and Annabel to catch up on logistics. They are keen for this to run for more than its allotted two nights but logistics of timetabling the stage are stretched. I will hope.

We have had four of the eight monologues so far – Paul's, Meera Syal's, Moira Buffini's and mine. They are all incredibly different. It is a practical reminder to me that storytelling is about controlling perspective. The more varied voices you have, the better it is.

In the evening Adrian and I go to the press night at the Old Vic of Joe Penhall's new play, *Mood Music*. It's an insightful discussion of who owns collaborative art. The cast were excellent, but the play didn't move me.

Friday 4 May

Lolita A day of meetings. The week is so short that when there's a day of meetings, I feel a whole writing day has been missed. Anyway, at least the meetings are positive.

The first one is for the MIF project. I meet the director, Leo Warner, who works in state of the art video projection. He explains the work of his company, 59 Productions, that he's built up over the last seventeen years. He wants everything to take place on a large scale. It's a site-specific, multidisciplinary production based on Italo Calvino's book *Invisible Cities* which is, basically, a conversation between Kublai Khan and Marco Polo. He wants to do it in a huge warehouse space in Manchester, then hopefully New York, Paris and Brisbane – incorporating digital projection, dance, music and text. It sounds very exciting. I tell him that I will read the book over the weekend, have a think and come back to them.

Then I meet with friend and artistic director of the Roundhouse, Marcus Davey. I've known Marcus for ten years and have always thought we would work together. He runs the Roundhouse with great humanity and ambition. It's a wonderful building and Adrian and I have been there often to watch, support and participate. I've had an idea for a piece of theatre for them, but it's taken me months to actually arrange this appointment. I am always nervous of starting something new because that's the easy bit. Once you start, you then have to follow through and that can take years.

We have lunch in Primrose Hill as the sun is shining. A good sign. He likes my idea. It would combine many storytelling elements that would include their young talent from the Roundhouse in a blending of professional and emerging artists. Anyway, it is lovely to see him and discuss how we finally might work together.

Katie, my literary agent, tells me the RSC are interested in *Pi*. They will have a planning meeting next week and discuss it.

Then I meet with a producer I worked with as an actress last year on *Delicious* for Sky TV. She is interested in my writing. We chat. I tell her an idea for a TV series that I've had for some time and she likes it. It's not formed yet, but I know it has huge potential. I tell her that I'll try and put it down on paper and we can progress from there. Television is the long game but she's a busy freelance producer and very clued up about screen work. So we'll see.

Home. The kids are both out tonight.

Adrian was filming but back for the evening. We have a rare night to ourselves.

Sunday 6 May

Lolita I'm at St Thomas' Hospital today observing the work of InterAct, a charity that supports survivors of strokes. Eighteen years ago, when I first started writing, an actress friend of mine told me that a new charity she was working for needed short stories to read in hospitals to stroke patients. They had a very particular remit: the pieces should be no more than three pages long and culturally varied. I was paid £200 a story. I had never been paid for writing before. I wrote forty stories for them over the next few years. Writing them allowed me to practise storytelling and I got honest feedback from the people who read them. It also supplemented my income for a while. Well, fast-forward eighteen years and I am now an ambassador for the charity, going in to support the great work they do.

Fellow ambassador Catherine McCormack and I are met at St Thomas' by Ulrika, who is one of the readers. She takes us up to the stroke rehabilitation ward and we watch her read and chat to a variety of patients for an hour. There are varying levels of responsiveness depending on the patients' condition but without exception, everyone is affected by Ulrika's reading and chat. It reminds me of the importance of direct human connection with another person.

I feel very comfortable in hospitals because of my dad being a doctor. I spent a lot of time in his hospital in Birmingham. I know they hold great struggle and suffering but the order and care is humbling. The patients here are very vulnerable but open to our visit. It is affirming to witness the power of words.

We are then taken for lunch by the heads of the charity to come up with ideas of how we might be able to help in the future.

Tuesday 8 May

Adrian   The Old Vic Theatre asked Lolita to curate a series of monologues to celebrate the seventy years that the NHS has been around and after a few conversations about the tone of the speeches, Lolita suggested me as director and the Old Vic have agreed.

For this performance the Old Vic want to capture a feeling of 'raw theatre'. One actor, one speech, no set, no props, just a voice and the audience. Today we are having a meeting to discuss how the pieces are coming along.

Eight writers are writing one monologue apiece, with each one covering a decade in the life of the Health Service.

Lolita has given them the remit to choose any topic and approach it from any angle. Until the pieces are written I can't enter into conversations on casting, or what the look and feel of the evening will be. I don't want to impose any ideas on it so will just wait and see what the pieces need. As usual, we can't do a thing without the words.

I've never directed theatre before, only TV and film. In those mediums, the performances and the story can be endlessly tweaked in an edit suite until you and the producers are happy with the finished product. There is so much control. You can get rid of bad moments in the script or an actor's performance or, conversely, you can spend more time with an actor that has given a more detailed and skillful performance than you imagined was in the script. In the theatre, although you may have weeks of rehearsal, what you get at the end is what you get. The actors and the writers are in control. Lolita has been in personal contact with each writer, looking at story ideas, meeting and working through the various drafts. I stand back and watch her work with each writer, offering notes to some while leaving others alone, measuring her response to each one based purely on what they need from her. I really don't think I have ever met anyone so organized and incredibly good at galvanizing and collaborating with those around her. I truly believe she would be a gift to any organization that asked her to take a managerial position.

We have been discussing the project at length and now that some drafts are beginning to come in, I have begun to have ideas about the look and feel of the performance.

Lolita is now working on the pieces of music that will link each monologue.

The writers are: Lolita, Moira Buffini, Courttia Newland, Meera Syal, Paul Unwin, Jack Thorne, Matilda Ibini and Seiriol Davies.

Meera's piece is beautiful, like a one-woman show. She walked in and delivered her first draft absolutely ready for rehearsal. It's very funny but delivers a gut punch to the Brexit xenophobia that trumpeted the idea that the NHS needed protecting from the scourge of immigrants. Paul's piece is direct address and takes a man from birth in the recent past to near death in a future without a health service. Moira's piece puts her mother, a dialysis nurse, on stage. It's direct address and is beautiful. Lolita's piece is drawn from her father's experience in the NHS and contains the most complicated medical knowledge of all the pieces. It's a surgeon engaged in a description of a hip operation to a younger colleague while at the same time recalling his training and early memories of being a doctor in Kolkata. The other writers are beginning to send in various drafts of their pieces.

I meet with Sophie Moniram, who is going to be my Associate Director on this project. All new territory for me. No form to follow here. I've just got to make sure everyone is on the same page and up to speed with what we aim to achieve on the nights.

I'm getting that familiar buzz I get when directing. I feel like all my faculties are engaged in this challenge. Eight actors, eight writers, eight monologues, eight songs, no set and very little rehearsal. I think the work will be really good.

After my meeting with Sophie, I head off to meet Simon Evans, Mike Poulton and James Bierman to talk about *Cyrano*.

Nearly two years ago, I received a new translation of *Cyrano De Bergerac* that had been written by Mike and was to be directed by Simon and produced by James. I wasn't aware of Simon and James' work at the time and although I really liked the version of the play, I didn't have the right gap in my diary to get involved and so I passed on the project, all the time thinking it would make a great show. It was just what I was looking for but the timing was wrong.

Anyway, time passes and eighteen months later I'm at the Donmar Warehouse watching Lenny Henry perform in *The Resistible Rise of Arturo Ui*. It's a great show. Very 'live' theatre. Actors are speaking directly to the audience – making them feel complicit in the plot of the play, making them vote with a show of hands and be involved with lines and decisions. It was very cleverly done, the audience at one point being invited to come sit on stage as a mark of how much they don't agree with what Arturo is doing. I was impressed by how tight the actors were as a team, really trusting each other with little bits of improv and songs. Speaking to Lenny afterwards, he tells me the director is well used to including the audience in performance as he is an expert magician who still performs now and then. It makes complete sense to me. I come away liking the fact that the audience went to the theatre to take part, not just sit back and be passively entertained.

Lenny puts me in touch with the director, who asks if we can meet and so the both of us are in polite contact until, one evening, I meet him at the house of a mutual friend. We get chatting about things we would love to do, I get on with him immediately, we promise to keep in touch and try to find something sometime.

On the way home, I keep thinking about *Cyrano*. Although I read that version well over a year ago, it won't leave my mind. Wrapped up in the opening scenes is everything that would bring the audience into the play. It is big and romantic and would serve me well, as I wanted to get back on stage but do something fun, not immerse myself in grief and tragedy again. I get home and check through my emails to find the play. I'm asking my agent to check with the producers to see if the part is still available.

It turns out that the play is still free and that the person who sent it to me nearly two years ago was the same guy who had directed Lenny at the Donmar, Simon Evans – the same person I thought would make a really good job of directing *Cyrano*.

We made contact again and, after a laugh, promised to get it on. Theatres have been contacted and have expressed strong interest. A couple of weeks ago, James organized a reading of the play for interested parties. It went well. The cast around the table were great and we now seem to have an embarrassment of options to chase. The one that makes us all keen is to go straight into the Theatre Royal Haymarket for a twelve-week run. It has recently been bought by a new company, headed by a CEO who loves the theatre. His development person came to the reading and liked what we did. He thinks the play will be a great success there.

So here are the four of us – Mike, Simon, James and myself – sitting around talking about how the reading went and sharing notes on the script. In these situations, it is always best if the writer hears one voice mainly give notes. For me, that is very much Simon's job as director. I had already given my notes to Simon, so he can then decide if they are relevant enough (or not) to give to Mike. We chatted for a while, sharing thoughts and changing each others minds with ideas that might work. The more we talk, the better the project feels. I can't wait to get started on it, not just because of Mike's excellent script, but because of the way we are already beginning to work. The relationships are clear and we're all pulling in the same direction. I just have to try and change the strong interest expressed by the theatres into firm commitments, but for some reason it doesn't seem to be happening yet. Most of the producers in London are very interested but have been reticent about moving forward with possible dates.

Lolita I spend the day writing the screenplay for *Red Velvet*. I am doing a round of notes that have been waiting since January sitting in my head, knocking – so it's very nice to finally get on with them.

These are thoughts Adrian gave me from the last version I did. He always looks at my writing with an actor's eye but also a directorial one. It's very useful because I come from an emotional logic rather than a visual one. I also have my own notes. The writing deadlines are stacking up a bit, so I need to finish this draft by the end of May.

I am booked to speak at the annual address for the Society of Theatre Research at the Art Workers' Guild in Bloomsbury. It is an audience of industry folk and academics. I think the Q&A went fine, though I am a bit tired as my head always gets foggy at the end of a writing day. As the session comes to a close, I can feel my fatigue and am bugged by that gentle insecurity that always follows an unprepared interview. They are a very nice group of people and hopefully I've said something interesting.

Wednesday 9 May

Adrian   Managed to get some writing on *Lottery Boy* done. Started trying to place the notes from my interviews with my police advisors into the script. I want to get an accurate picture of what it's like to deal with street level crime in the city. How do the gangs work? What might my lead character have to endure? The legal highs, dog-fighting, prostitution, the terminology and finally, the methods the police use to deal with it all?

During the interviews with both my advisors, I was surprised and saddened by the facts and scenarios they put forward. The level of depravity out there ready to swallow vulnerable people is shocking. It's not just about need, it's a focused, calculated cruelty based purely on money, sex and power. The advisors told me these facts with a nod and a little shrug. It is what it is, criminals will ruthlessly destroy a vulnerable life to make a profit. They always have and always will. Children used for sex. Old people manipulated for whatever money they have. As long as the target seems weak and unable to defend itself properly, there is some sort of profit that can be made. Perhaps I sound a little naive, but it made me angry.

Anger is a great place to write from. Both my advisors, though matter of fact, were aware of the power they had as officers. They took real pride in what the uniform stands for, pride in the fact that 90 per cent of their work keeps the public safe everyday and takes place in the unreported and unnoticed areas of London's crime scene. I began to have lots of ideas while talking to them but as I began to insert those ideas into the script, I saw that I have simply pulled it apart and made it loose and heavy. This script that I had worked so hard to make tight, dramatic and moving, now, with lots of shocking moments attached to facts and figures, had become flabby and portentous. It's not a documentary. I have to trust the intelligence of the audience that will watch the film, and allow them to fill in the gaps and use their imagination.

My office looks like a modern art installation. Over 300 white postcards with various bits of scrawl are spread out geometrically on my floor, one card for every scene in the film, different colours for each character. This is me doing things old school so that I can see at a glance how long a character has been off screen, what their next plot moment could or should be, how they serve the whole story etc. It's probably not a good idea to own up to this but – I don't have much of an idea about acts, turning points and inciting incidents. I've learned everything I know as a director and writer by meticulously studying other people's work while I've been involved in it. I read back over my script and end up taking out a hell of a lot of what I had just spent hours putting in. Feels like I've wasted the day . . . five steps forward, three steps back.

Thursday 10 May

Adrian   I'm on set for *The Rook* with director Kari Skogland, doing a love scene with Gina McKee. It's nice getting to work with an actor you have admired over the years in various performances. In that awkward quiet before the cameras rolled, as she sat straddling me for our sex scene I politely told her that I'd always wanted to work with her. She said 'yeah, me too', and then we burst out laughing. After plotting what we were going to do for each moment in the scene, we made quick work of getting it shot. Personally, I don't like it when directors try to get you to just improvise having sex and then try to shoot it from a discreet angle. The problem is it makes you increasingly self-conscious, because you become aware of everything you are pretending to do and get more and more tense. It's always best, as we did in this case, to work out exactly what moves should be made at each moment and repeat it again and again for every angle. In this way the camera can capture the full scene with all the little details, plus the exact repetition and choreography protects the actors' sensibilities. Happily it's becoming the norm that scenes of this nature aren't shot from a male perspective.

This particular scene was a tricky one to get right for the episode, as it's how our characters are introduced to the audience. An awful lot had to be established in our very first moments on screen. Even so, Kari managed to convey all of this while setting the first scene so that it played in one seemingly simple, but technically complicated, shot. A very good move. I'm a fan of Kari's work on *The Handmaid's Tale* and so watching her work on set gave me an opportunity to observe and take note.

Friday 11 May

Adrian   Off to the Old Vic this morning to rehearse for their 200th birthday celebrations. Said yes before I'd really thought about it but now I'm glad I did. Tim Minchin is setting a world record by singing *200 Green Bottles Standing on a Wall* with a cast of what seems like hundreds of people and has arranged a *Singin' in the Rain* segment to go along with it. Damian Lewis, Bertie Carvel and I are going to soft-shoe our way through it and have turned up today to learn the choreography. Tim Minchin is sat quietly beside our director Matthew Warchus having a listen and watching the start of the rehearsal. Every time I've seen Tim perform, he has been incredible. He's a bit of a genius and now here I am meeting him with Damian and Bertie. I manage to keep my over-eager excitement under wraps and remain professional. Funny how people who work in this world get star-struck meeting other people who work in this world too.

Home and off to a Taekwondo class. It's very nice to get my head into another zone and switch off. One of the other black belts, Uguz Kazim, worked our arms until I thought they would fall off. It's always at this point that the voice in your head starts making excuses, encouraging you to stop and give up. When we all needed a rest, he handed the class over to me. After a quick break I took everyone through some basic *nunchaku* and *bō* staff techniques, all the while trying to remember the choreography I had worked on at the theatre.

Lolita   I agree to be the writer on the MIF project. I will be adapting Italo Calvino's *Invisible Cities*.

Contemplating working on this scale is blowing my mind. It's not an instantly theatrical piece and talks about reality versus dreams, truth versus fiction. A lot of it reads through a cloud of opium, which gives you an idea of what it's like. Anyway I said yes. So it's real.

I do my redraft of 'Speedy Gonzalez', my piece for *The Greatest Wealth*. I am pleased with it. It says what I want to say now. A few tweaks and it will be done.

I have a call with one of the other writers for *The Greatest Wealth* and feed back on her first draft. At the same time I am fielding emails about casting. We got Gloria Obianyo, which is great news. We were just in *Fanny and Alexander* together. She's a great actress but also a fantastic singer. She is going to be our lone singing voice between the monologues – setting the scene for each decade.

Then I continue writing *Red Velvet*. I've done the initial notes and am tightening it up now. It's amazing how long it takes to say what you really mean. I'm halfway through now. Hopefully I'll be able to send Ken Branagh a draft by the end of next week (he's interested in producing the film). I am writing him a part in the film – Edmund Kean. Edmund was in the early drafts of the play but I had to cut him out because he didn't serve the narrative in the end. I loved him as character: he's fiery, visceral, rude, drunk. It's very satisfying to put him back in.

I go to pick my daughter up from an after-school thing and sit reading *Invisible Cities* in the car.

In the evening I am tempted to keep working but my brain hurts. I want to realize what is emerging in my head but of course, that will take time.

I force myself to switch off and watch TV.

Sunday 13 May

Adrian   12.00 pm. Off to the Old Vic to join Damian and Bertie for another rehearsal for the celebrations. The three of us got on stage, tried out our steps. Seems to work. I think it'll be fun. We'll see what the real thing is like tonight.

Lolita   10.00 pm. This evening Adrian and I are at the bicentenary gala dinner for the Old Vic.

It is a unique affair – red carpet on the way into the theatre with interviews along the way. We meet Danny Sapani on the way in. I don't think I've ever worked with Danny but we've known each other for many years and have been acting for the same amount of time.

It is interesting when we do an interview on the way in. I can feel the fundamental shift that is happening within the industry and the wider world in regards to the #MeToo and Time's Up campaigns and the conversations and actions taking place regarding diversity.

On the red carpet an interviewer asks Danny, Adrian and me a question about the current changes in the industry. I am so used to standing back and not being asked my opinion but tonight I am invited to speak. The change they are referring to is the exposure of sexual harassment and exploitation within the industry. They need a woman to answer that. It feels like a seismic shift. There are many compromises we live under as women but this one took me by surprise. You only get the chance to speak if people want to hear your answer. It's that simple. When people are only interested in one point of view and you don't fit that demographic, it feels futile to try to join the conversation. You ask yourself, why speak if no one is interested in your voice?

The event is great. Tim Minchin set a world record of singing *200 Green Bottles* live on stage with many special guests. Adrian, Damian Lewis and Bertie Carvel did a cool singing and dancing segment which went well. There was an amazing line-up of stars involved. The theatre has been transformed into a dining room.

What really strikes me about this event is its message. The Old Vic, until very recently, felt like a bastion of old values to me and a bit of a closed shop. But last year I auditioned at the Old Vic for the first time in my twenty-eight-year career. I got the job and was in *Fanny and Alexander*. Seeing the programme of entertainment tonight, I am hopeful that the change is real and permanent. There is pure diversity at the absolute heart of the evening. It's not advertised, not sold, not demonstrated, but there are all kinds of people on that stage. We have a preview of Kate Prince's piece *Sylvia*, about the suffragettes. It is an exhilarating piece of work. I see many friends and colleagues here tonight. I am reminded that acting and writing is part of a wide community. I'm very lucky to be part of it.

Adrian Midnight. Damian, Bertie and I had to come on from the side of the stage at a specific point in the music, hit our marks, work in sync with tap steps and the vocals then get off stage at the right beat for the other dancers to come on. I'm very disappointed in myself as I missed a few steps. Lolita tells me it's hardly noticeable but I like to count myself as a mover and couldn't keep time to all of it. It went by so quickly. Got feedback when I hit my long notes . . . unfortunate. Still, it worked overall in the end. Great finish by Tim Minchin. One of the best fundraisers of its kind that I have seen – exuberant, honest, awash with talent and full of feeling. I might have a bit of a headache tomorrow.

Tuesday 15 May

Lolita Back to writing today. The *Red Velvet* screenplay is coming together but just as the overall arc of this version starts to reveal itself, it disappears into the dark, out of focus and I have to find it. Not always sure what I'm doing – feels like excavating with a very small archeological brush, trying to find the story's bones. When I have moments of doubt I walk away, get some air, and then come back to continue dusting away at the rock face.

I start work on *Invisible Cities*. I mark up the novel for the words and phrases that tell me the story. Then I type them up – this is my starting point.

It's what I did with *Pi* – but I loved the novel of *Life of Pi*, having read it many years before taking it on as an adaptation, whereas I don't know Calvino's work, and this book in many ways seems impenetrable. What is interesting, though, is that as I follow my instincts and type up the words, the story starts to reveal itself – not so much a narrative but an essence.

Writing is so delicate. I find myself following a scent and hoping it leads somewhere. It does. But then I doubt it and have to walk away and return only when the negative voices in my head stop.

I finish my monologue for *The Greatest Wealth* today and send it off to the producers at the Old Vic and Adrian. It finally says what I want it to. It's about working in the NHS whilst knowing what life is like without it. My dad talks about the lack of facilities in India all the time – I think it tells a good story. It feels good to have that off my plate.

Am pinging emails back and forth to the Old Vic about casting. It is exciting to be a part of that conversation and to have a strong steer on it.

I also speak to Helen at InterAct, the stroke charity. When I met them a few days ago, I had a lot of creative ideas that needed further explanation. Helen told me that they want to increase their visibility so she is exploring all possibilities. As I talk to her, I realize how much I know and how long I've been around, from running Ensemble Theatre Company with Adrian in the early 1990s to producing a short film and a charity gala, to casting, writing and rehearsing. Our work is so disjointed that it can be hard to piece together a whole career from all its composite parts. Sometimes I forget how much I have done.

In the evening, I meet with some of the actors from *Hamlet* to see Caroline Martin (who was our Horatia) in *Way of the World* at the Donmar. It is a good production, and the actors work hard with such a dense text. I sometimes wonder at the relevance of these old classics – it's an age-old question. As I sit alone in my office and try to tell stories, I am constantly questioning why. What is the relevance of this story now? When I see old plays that seem to have no relevance to today's world, it makes me wonder – am I too literal? Does it have to matter? Isn't pure entertainment good enough? Taste is such an unquantifiable thing. What makes you like one thing and not another?

Too many questions. It is a lovely night. I have drinks with Caroline and the girls and catch up on all their busy lives. A wonderful group of women.

Thursday 17 May

Adrian   Back on set shooting *The Rook*. I have scenes with Olivia Munn today and found out she has a black belt in Taekwondo. She said she hadn't got a gym here yet or a trainer, and that she would love to do a class or get some training together. Great idea. But I suddenly felt that for this Hollywood actress, travelling for an hour to get to a community centre in south-east London might not be quite what she had in mind. It started me thinking, though. It'd be really good for us to get a site-specific venue that stores all the weapons and equipment we need for our classes; a place with the space to invite other practitioners to run classes at different times of the day. Then the PE sessions that are attended by schools, yoga teaching, general self-defence classes and personal trainers could all have timetabled use of the same space. A room like that is going to be difficult to find in London.

Lolita   Cross-eyed in front of my computer today.

Juggling writing, emails and rejections!

I am writing *Red Velvet*, putting in arcs for my main characters, beats that are missing. I am not on form. It is slow.

Endless emails come in about *The Greatest Wealth* – casting suggestions, questions about rehearsal times. I got Jack Thorne's piece for the 1940s. It is beautifully written for a deaf actress to perform almost entirely in sign. It's an unexpected 'voice' and so good. I have a minor suggestion in terms of clarity and Jack was very responsive to it. Jack is inspiring: to have so much experience and success and still listen to someone you've just met is impressive. This Old Vic project will be short lived but burn very bright.

I have some bad news. In 2016 I was part of a writers' room for a new series for the BBC. I spent five weeks in that room with some wonderful writers. I wrote an episode and then did another draft. The project was delayed. Now it is about to get green-lit and I hear they don't want me to continue. They are giving it to another writer.

These things happen, I know, but what frustrates me is that I had received minimal notes and written the next draft, after which I'd had no contact for over a year. It was on the basis of that draft that I was asked to step down.

On the one hand, at the Old Vic my opinion is valued and on the other, I'm dispensable. This industry baffles me. Treating people without care becomes acceptable. Hope I'm never like that.

Try to focus back on my writing but find it hard.

Friday 18 May

Adrian   Off to Birmingham to see family.

Interesting to read in Anthony Burgess' introduction to *Cyrano de Bergerac* of his director's problems with the story. They're exactly the same areas of fairy tale and disbelief that I have a problem with when I read it. It's ok to stick a classic on stage. But the bits that inevitably don't work have to be wrestled with. Leaving them alone with a kind of 'well, that's the play' attitude does nothing for a modern audience with modern sensibilities who have paid to enjoy the story. No matter how old it is, it has to follow logic.

Lolita   Art Malik has accepted the part in my monologue for the Old Vic. Art Malik, who I would watch on the big screen as a teenager in Birmingham. Who was the British Asian presence on TV at a time when there was virtually no one.

The business still charms me occasionally. In the midst of all the graft and disappointments and petty judgements and frustrations are moments like this, when someone you admired as a kid comes and works with you because you have written a story they can tell.

Sunday 20 May

Adrian Reached Birmingham for a visit with my mum and see some family but felt a little guilty that I immediately had to sit down and get *Lottery Boy* off to my producers Jeffrey Sharp and Luke Redgrave. I had slogged away at it on the train and now wanted to let it go. There has to be an end to the wrestling with scenes and a character's point of view. It gets to a point where you could spend months tweaking.

Everything always seems smaller at my mum's place. My memories of being a child around the same furniture always hits me. I sat at the table and disappeared into my script. Got it done in the early hours and sent it off.

As I did so, I noticed open folders on my computer full of notes that I had promised myself I would pull together into a series idea that I wanted to approach the people at Sky with. I should collate that material together and create a pitch document. But not now. I closed my laptop and headed off to bed. No work for a couple of days.

Lolita I read poems for Amnesty's Women Making History Festival in Shoreditch. I am on stage with Juliet Stevenson, Indira Varma and Olivia Colman. We each read a couple of poems for an audience to celebrate women.

We are all a bit nervous – these things are always a balance of relaxed and performed, unrehearsed and polished. You turn up as yourself and have to present.

In the 1980s when I was a schoolgirl in Birmingham, my school took us to a poetry reading by actors from the RSC. In my memory it was in a stately home, maybe a gallery, a smart room. There were four actors and two of them I remember vividly: they were Alan Rickman and Juliet Stevenson. All my friends and I thought they were both fantastic. I was very inspired by the way they turned poetry into performance and feeling. Standing here with Juliet I remember how I felt watching her as a teenager.

Monday 21 May

Lolita   Have a meeting this morning with the director, designer and producer from 59 Productions at Rambert Dance on the South Bank. We chat about *Invisible Cities* and the parameters of the project so far.

It will have twenty or thirty dancers from Rambert. Sidi Larbi Cherkaoui is choreographing it. We talk about the book, which is in turns brilliant and frustrating in its pseudo mysticism. The Western representation of Eastern philosophy can grate on me. It can be cloaked in an observer's coat, which makes it exoticized. Whilst some of the book is scratching at genuinely existential questions, some of it is obtuse.

We talk about the cities and what they represent and it is fascinating to hear their plans, ideas and vision for this piece. It's going to be big and international. The canvas is vast and all stems from the story. So my job now is to come up with story that has purpose.

Wednesday 23 May

Lolita   Have a meeting this morning with director Max Webster and producer Simon Friend about *Pi*.

We hadn't sat down and talked through things since the workshop last month, so it is good to catch up. We are waiting to see if the RSC might jump on board with us. That would be the best scenario because their infrastructure would totally support development and production. We have other theatres fully behind it, so are working out what would be the best option. It is nice to chat about it all before I jump into the redraft tomorrow.

I am timetabling work for next year that will require my full attention. *Invisible Cities* has sent an initial schedule for May to July next year and *Pi* looks to be either the same time or in the autumn. If it's at the RSC, we'll have to see what slot they have.

These feel like big conversations that all hinge on the script. Sobering. I spend the afternoon putting things in order, catching up with *The Greatest Wealth* – casting and reading a couple of new drafts for the monologues.

Tidy up my notes from the *Invisible Cities* meeting and look at 59 Productions' past work to get an idea of what digital media they are capable of.

Get my notes out for *Pi* to start tomorrow.

By the way, yesterday I finished the draft of *Red Velvet* and sent it to Ken Branagh. It's imperfect but good and I'm ready to have another set of eyes on it.

I also got an acting job – *Riviera*, season two. Adrian was in season one and directed two episodes and his character died in Episode 9. I just have three episodes, but it will be fun. Light but high drama and it films in Nice.

Friday 25 May

Lolita   It is a dizzying day. Mostly because I am aware the girls have a half-day at school before breaking up for half term and it is hard to concentrate when they are at home. Kids require time. It is nice to hang out with them but everything you need to focus on gets shunted to the back of the brain queue.

I had wanted to start *Pi* yesterday – but didn't. Got diverted reading a script for a possible acting job, giving notes on a monologue, tax, calls and emails followed by a meeting with Adrian and Tina Price, our publicist. We've known her for over twenty years and she has always done our PR. But this is a new incarnation of our lives together. She is going to be our personal manager. She will be in charge of our diaries, coordinate any requests and invitations, organize our attendance at anything to do with work. She is very efficient and knows us extremely well, but it requires a transfer of much more information so that we can establish her new position.

MIF is planning a research and development trip for key creatives to Venice next week, so I hand that over to Tina to manage the travel details.

Then we continue the meeting, timetabling our various projects and any crossovers we have to avoid.

So the day is done. It is half term.

Next week is busy with work but the girls are prepping for summer exams. Adrian's schedule is up in the air and the deals have not been done for me acting in *Riviera* for Sky or writing for MIF. Also I have this possibility of another TV writing job.

All of my work revolves around me and my ideas. Part of me thinks the chaos of life informs the work and gives it edge. The other part thinks it disrupts the peace from which ideas can flow. Which is right?

Saturday 26 May

Adrian Monologues for *The Greatest Wealth* are coming in and being given notes by Lolita and the team. We have asked Jenny Peters, a long-time friend of ours who worked with Lolita as an actress, and has since stepped away from the profession to become a British Sign Language interpreter, to sign each of our monologues in performance. She hasn't signed theatre before, so this will be a first for her too.

Jack Thorne's piece came in – it is called 'BOO'. We will need a Deaf actress to perform it, signing her way through the piece and will now need Jenny to give 'voice' to the character (a bit like an inner monologue). Jenny is being slowly coaxed back to speaking as an actress on stage.

In order to make this piece work, I'm going to need the actress to translate Jack's words into British Sign Language and then have Jenny watch her and translate her movements back into spoken English, all while trying to keep as many of Jack's words as possible. This is going to be interesting.

Matilda Ibini's piece has also come in. It will require an actress who is a wheelchair-user to perform it. Normally on a performance you would work with one writer. We're working with eight. And it's all untested new material.

I suppose I should accept the 'off the cuff' raw nature of *The Greatest Wealth* performances. I should accept it as a series of rough-and-ready, script-in-hand, organic speeches . . . but I'm not going to. It is a show. A performance in appreciation of the NHS. Even if it's new material and we have very little rehearsal with a very small budget, it's still a performance and I'll direct it as such.

Tuesday 29 May

Lolita   I do a reading today at the Park Theatre for a new play. It's an interesting piece set a little in the future where they have 'solved' the issue of too many old people using up our resources. It's well written. A cast of five very experienced actors. We do a gentle read-through in the morning and then a performance read to an invited audience in the afternoon. It always amazes me what an audience brings out in actors; they make us rise to a performance and tell the story with detail and emotion.

Afterwards I meet up with Adrian in the West End for the press night of *Consent*, a really interesting piece about sexual politics, power and relationships. Great performances and beautiful writing.

Friday 1 June

Lolita   I arrived in Venice yesterday afternoon. I'm on a research trip for *Invisible Cities* with Leo and Jenny from 59 and Benoit, the acting director of Rambert. We're staying at a hotel next to the Rialto Bridge. My room is tiny but perfectly formed.

Today we all meet up and go to the architectural Biennale in the Giardini. It is fascinating to consider space, light, perspective, shape and structure. *Invisible Cities* is about all of these things and Venice runs through all of the novel.

The Biennale is so interesting. Exhibitions by different countries focusing on specific aspects of space, architecture and use. There are some incredibly clever pieces that really make me think. One exhibition is full of the same kitchen repeated again and again in different perspectives. I feel like Alice in Wonderland as I enter through a tiny door into one tiny kitchen then a giant door to another bigger kitchen. It is magical and fun.

One project shows affordable housing and what different people have done with the same minimal space. There are exact models of their homes and all the details within them as well as videos of the actual spaces and the people who live there.

Jenny, Leo and Benoit are lovely people and it is so interesting to hear about their work and artistic disciplines. I have no inside knowledge of dance, digital projection, design, architecture – all of these perspectives are in *Invisible Cities*. Really informative.

We have lunch and then I go back to the hotel to work on the storyline of the piece. The book is expansive in that it is full of visual imagery but it has no story – so I was a bit cross-eyed by the end of the afternoon. I did some useful work. I think I need to chip away at my instinctive response to the book until the story reveals itself.

I meet with Leo, Jenny and Benoit for dinner and we have interesting chats. It's my birthday today. I'm forty-nine. I have had lots of lovely texts and calls from nearest and dearest.

Saturday 2 June

Lolita   Spend the morning with Leo and Jenny at the Doge's Palace. Great to see epic halls, paintings, statues, columns, windows, doors. All very resonant of *Invisible Cities*.

When I came here on Thursday, I had no storyline for the book – it was a daunting prospect trying to work my way into some sort of narrative. I leave having etched out a storyline.

Being amongst the winding streets and canals of Venice while I write this story, which is wrapped up in memory and streets, has been brilliant. Every second place here is named after Marco Polo and here I am imagining him. I have talked architecture, form and space and dance (things I knew little about) – it has been immeasurably helpful. Even the feeling of walking through a low and dark alley of wonky houses into a surprisingly light square has been very valuable to this process.

Tuesday 5 June

Lolita   I write *Pi* today.

The clock is ticking as *The Greatest Wealth* starts to gather steam and *Riviera* have booked me. I have to go to Nice to film next week.

All this other work breaks my writing concentration. It makes me work more intently, though. The minutes I spend at my computer are pure and full. I get to the interval of *Pi* just marking my way through the new structure from the notes and discoveries I made from the workshop.

It's hard work and every few minutes I walk away from the computer to think and then go back and write. The structure is good. Max's questions and guidance were really strong.

All day I am fielding emails regarding *The Greatest Wealth* and casting. I ask my dear friend Louise English if she would do Seiriol Davies' musical monologue. She's an amazing all-rounder – singer, dancer, performer. She says yes. I am thrilled.

We also get Ruth Madeley, who Adrian is working with on *The Rook*. So our cast is complete and they are amazing – experienced, diverse and so talented. I feel proud. Very glad to have stuck to my instincts, grateful to the Old Vic for having been so open and facilitating these choices.

I go to the Bridge Theatre in the evening with Adrian to see *My Name is Lucy Barton*. I have a coughing fit halfway through and have to leave. I watch it on the TV monitor outside. Laura Linney is very charismatic and watchable – even on this small screen.

Friday 8 June

Adrian   First rehearsals today for *The Greatest Wealth* with David Threlfall, Paul Unwin and Meera Syal. All went really well. Used the time to read through the pieces, cut what was unnecessary and change what was unclear. They were all very good about the cuts I suggested, adding lots of their own. Meera did both jobs herself as she has written her own piece. Great watching her read it through in character, then stop to cut and change the words before sounding it out again. A novelist, actress, comedian, writer with a great singing voice, one day she'll get the credit she truly deserves in this industry. After that, I went on to a production meeting. We all sit round a table and quickly introduce ourselves stating what department we are from and what we will be doing in the show. Half an hour later while we discuss projections and sound, I've got no idea of anyone's names and have lost track of which department each person is from when I talk to them.

Brilliant.

Monday 11 June

Lolita   I fly to Nice this morning.

I am filming *Riviera* for Sky Atlantic. I was driven straight to set and spent the next four hours in hair and make-up. Very nice people but four hours is pushing my limits. I look very swish by the end, of course –glam and effortless!

A long drive back to the hotel.

I can't do any more writing in the evening. My brain is too fractured by different things – details of *The Greatest Wealth*, interviews and photos being planned, lines to learn for tomorrow's filming and thoughts from other writing jobs. I did start reading *The Writer* by Ella Hickson. I missed it when it was on at the Almeida (a friend of mine was in it) a few weeks back. It's brilliant. So clever, funny and true.

Tuesday 12 June

Lolita   It is my first day of shooting today. For some reason, I am quite nervous. I know the lines backwards but am getting worried I don't. It's that feeling of being unfamiliar with the way they work and the mood on set and not wanting to be the person who slows it all down. I didn't, of course. It is fine. And once I've done the first scene and my lines are attached to characters and action, it goes smoothly.

Not having faces and relationships in your head makes acting recitation. What makes it acting is the fact that you say the words with underlying intention and history. It's all about the exchange with other people and your surroundings. It's all about relationships.

I was told at drama school that it takes ten years at least to make a good actor. I remember being shocked that it would take that long. Of course once I reached ten years, I started to realize it takes a lifetime and more. Because ultimately acting is not a skill you achieve it is an evolving ever-changing discipline. It can never be mastered.

We overrun by almost two hours. It was almost 1.00 am when I finish.

Wednesday 13 June

Lolita   Today is full on. I wake up in Nice, have breakfast and go to the airport.

Have a call just before take off from producer Simon about *Pi*. The RSC have offered us a slot next March but Max isn't free. We are talking about possibilities of splitting rehearsal time. Amazing to have an offer though (almost – we have to wait a couple of weeks for certainty). I have to hang up as we are literally about to take off.

As I fly back to London, I write *Pi*.

Get picked up at the airport and driven to the Old Vic for an afternoon of press for *The Greatest Wealth*. I had emailed Adrian to bring me a change of clothes for a photo, because I only found out about this when I was in Nice and didn't have anything. He's been running around with rehearsals and shooting. So I get my clothes from him and went to change but realized that he hadn't brought what I'd asked for. I'm having a photo for the *Daily Telegraph* and I have to make the best of what I have on.

I am feeling a little rattled and tired from last night's shoot.

Anyway, me and my dad have pictures in the bar upstairs. The piece is about me growing up as a doctor's daughter. There will be a current picture of me and my dad, as well as old photos too. He brings a great selection to choose from. He's never done anything like this before in his eighty-four years. He's quite shy really but he did really well. Tina, our publicist, takes very good care of us both and then gets him a car home.

Then I do a phone interview for the article. Someone is going to ghost-write as me but I will get approval.

Then Adrian and I do an interview with a journalist for the *Today* programme. It is fine, but we can tell she is looking for an angle. It always feels like criticism rather than interest. At one point she calls us 'leftie luvvies'. I've been called many things in my time but that is a first. When did that happen? When did I stop being on the outside and suddenly become part of the establishment? Hilarious.

Then Adrian and I do a bit of filming for the Old Vic's social media site. By now I am starting to waffle and the words don't connect. Apparently it is okay, so I have to trust that, but I am feeling tired, exposed and inarticulate.

I have loved curating *The Greatest Wealth* and I love that it is something people will want to see but the exposure of it, of standing behind a public event is uncomfortable. You become management in a different sort of way.

Louise English came to the theatre to rehearse her piece with Adrian. I stayed and watched rehearsal for a little bit. Adrian has wanted to direct theatre for years. He understands the words from inside out. It's great watching him work on all these very different pieces. Louise was just great. Seiriol Davies' writing is weighty but fun and wicked. It all lifted my spirits. Louise always makes me laugh. And then I got a cab home.

Had a chat on the phone with Max about the RSC possibility for *Pi*. All very exciting, but not quite right in terms of his availability. Just have to see how this plays out.

Adrian I've now been in rehearsal with Dervla Kirwan, Moira Buffini, Seiriol Davies, Louise English, Sophie Stone and Jenny Peters. I'm liking the different perspectives on the NHS. The different positions the writers have taken.

I suppose story is perspective, really. If we keep looking at our history and our present from the same point of view, our stories will dry up and we'll end up repeating ourselves, then any act of storytelling becomes one of nostalgia. It's good to see that these monologues will be anything but that.

Saturday 16 June

Adrian Went up to Manchester in the morning to take part in a photo shoot for Sky's drama *Curfew*, a series I completed (as an actor) earlier in the year. It is set in a dystopian parallel reality where everyone lives under a totalitarian government controlled by a multinational corporation. The title comes from the fact that when it gets dark, people lock their doors and roll down their metal shutters because the beasts (flesh-eating human hybrids) come out at night. In order to escape this nightmare world, members of the public enter an illegal street race to the death where the winner gets to leave Britain and live somewhere safe. I play the father of a teenager that has broken the law and might 'disappear' if I don't do something to get him and my family to safety. So, we enter the street race in a tricked-out Volvo estate. It's a mad-genius idea for a series, throwing together lots of popular film genres, very bold with lots of action. I have no idea how this will go down with the TV audience.

It was nice to see the cast again and hear how the story had developed since my character had, erm, 'left the screen'.

Being away from home at certain periods can be costly on care for the family. I try to reduce it as much as possible and squeeze things together. If I'm not around, I force parenting onto Lolita who has to manage while working her projects. The same is true for her with me.

So after the shoot I put on a suit and jump into a car to Sheffield to attend the Royal Sparkle Sheffield Autism Awards, a charity founded by Liesje Dusauzay to help children and young people with autism and provide support for their families. The ceremony is attended by the current Lord Mayor of Sheffield, Magid Magid, as well as John Holt, the Vice Lord-Lieutenant of South Yorkshire, and the many councillors who have been Mayor at one time or another: they call themselves 'The Chain Gang'.

I give out an award for sibling of the year – children who at eight, ten and thirteen years old had become the primary source of support and care for their autistic brother or sister. I read testimonies from grateful parents, impressed teachers and friends. Very moving stuff. The kids are fantastic. I pose for selfies, congratulate Liesje on what she has managed to put together for hers and other people's children and talk to representatives of the council and the hotel thanking them for supporting her. An evening where I got to meet some great people who are working hard to help others. I'm really glad I was able to make the ceremony.

Then at 11.00 pm I jumped into a car to get back to London. Tomorrow is Father's Day and I fully intend to milk it.

Monday 18 June

Lolita　Had a turgid day today. Had too little sleep last night and so my thought processes were slow.

I sit down to write *Pi* when the girls went to school around 7.30 am. I am looking and looking at it and not solving anything easily. I crawl through my work then go out for a walk to post a letter, get some air and clear my head.

Days like this happen but I get frustrated when I'm not efficient. Time is so short between managing kids, life, acting and writing, that I need to be efficient.

I feel incredibly disheartened. In order to come up with the work that is necessary to solve all of the problems that have been presented to me, I need more rest and a degree of openness to allow new thoughts to form. When those elements are missing, I find it difficult.

I make a list. That's what I do when I feel discouraged.

I trace back a year to the day and list the things that have happened in between. When I make lists like this I can see what I've done in the year and can also spot positive or negative patterns.

I see that in the last year all of my acting has been achieved but half of my writing has either gotten stalled or ditched. There is a truth in what I am feeling – I'm working as hard as I can right now, but a lot of what I'm doing remains unfulfilled. Studying the list makes sense of my current lack of enthusiasm and frustration. Here I am again, answering questions and solving character's problems all the while feeling like the work I put in is futile.

Days like this are trying.

Tuesday 19 June

Lolita I write for an hour and a half this morning. It is much better than yesterday. Funny how on some days clarity shows itself and other days it hides.

I am in the second half of *Pi* on the lifeboat, taking out a lot of characters because he needs to be alone. It's coming along – slowly, slowly. In my mind I feel a loose end waiting for the RSC to make their decision. What if . . .?

Then I put my actress head on, get myself ready for an audition and head into town.

It's for an Amazon Prime series. It's a nice part. I didn't have time to learn it but I'm familiar with it and I'm at an age now where I feel this isn't a memory test, it's about the performance. So I don't stress.

The audition goes well, I think. I have been seen by this casting director a fair few times and never get the job but for me the audition is fine. I am present and I played it. Auditions are tricky. If you want the job too much or really haven't prepared enough, it all affects your performance. You have a twenty-minute window for them to see who you are and what you can do but also to show your ability to yourself.

There's nothing worse than wasting an audition. Now I try to do my best for me and if I get the job, great; if I don't, at least I practised my acting.

Saturday 23 June

Adrian   Just took part in a Talk Radio interview for *The Greatest Wealth*. As I check through other interviews and opinions about the NHS, I'm struck by the people who seem to have lost sight of just how incredible the concept is – that binding, all-inclusive idea to provide support to an entire country with health care. It leaves me speechless when I'm asked to come up with some kind of justification for the service. How can this country's greatest achievement need any kind of justification?

Maybe I'm being naive. We all know it needs fixing. I think everyone accepts that fact. I'm just a bit lost for words when people ask me to justify the idea itself.

Monday 25 June

Adrian   The *Rook* production team have worked the schedule so that I can be away from the shoot for the next week in order to give me the space to tech and dress *The Greatest Wealth*.

Tech for the first half starts at 10.00 am, then we do a dress at 3.30 pm, then the first performance. All in one day. I'm hoping the actors pace themselves. The crew at the theatre, led by Alex Constantin, are great. They're plotting and sorting out the sound without having really hung lights or set mics specifically for us. They're kind of using what they've got in the space already. This works out fine and each piece is given a technical work through before a run of the monologue. Every actor creates and inhabits the world on their own. Their confidence and belief in themselves is the currency I trade in. Any ideas I have must increase that confidence. No matter how good an idea is, if the actor has to stop and reach for it to make it work, it's a bad idea and interrupts the flow of what they're trying to achieve. I have to walk along with them through the piece and remove the things that stop them getting completely lost in the world they have created.

The tech is smooth and the show is received well. I'm incredibly nervous in the theatre watching them. Willing them, after such little rehearsal, to get everything right. I now know why so many directors never watch their first nights. The evening is a success, and the audience response at the end is really nice to hear. Tears, laughter and cheering. Sophie Stone, David Threlfall, Meera Syal, Dervla Kirwan and Gloria Obianyo are excellent.

Lolita I go to the Old Vic at lunchtime. They'd been teching all morning. The stage looks great. They've kept the thrust stage of the last show, *Mood Music*, and it makes the space very intimate. We have a single piano, a clothing rail and a chair. The remit of the evening is to be minimal but that can be freeing. Adrian chose simple things that tell story. It looks simple but classy.

The actors are nervous, tired but focused and working hard. The dress is fine. Difficult to talk to a theatre when there's no one there.

The show goes up at 8.30 pm and goes well.

It's such an eclectic, unusual and interesting evening. Sophie Stone performs Jack Thorne's monologue set in the 1940s in sign language with Jenny Peters voicing it. Then, for the 1950s, David Threlfall travels a whole life from birth to death into the future as written by Paul Unwin. Meera Syal performs the piece she has written about a midwife in 1960s Wolverhampton after Enoch Powell's 'Rivers of Blood' speech. And finally Dervla Kirwan gives Moira Buffini's words eloquence and feeling in 1970s England. All of it is tied together by Gloria Obianyo's beautiful voice and presence and Dylan Townley's effortless piano playing.

I feel very proud. Adrian has done a lovely job directing it.

I am sent my next script for *Riviera*. Lovely, glam, elusive. It's always strange to move from the deep involvement in writing to playing a part you're given. Very different levels of engagement.

Tuesday 26 June

Adrian Back at the Old Vic at 10.00 am to do the whole thing all over again, but this time with the second half.

It's much the same deal only as we go through the plotting, I realize that this is the half that has had even less rehearsal than the first half.

I'm having to make decisions in the tech that were never sorted in the rehearsal room.

The dress goes well. I am in awe at some of the actors, knowing that if I were in their position I wouldn't be able to do what they have just done.

The performance is good, very strong. A couple of line calls but they did really well. Audience response was loud and proud.

Lolita   I go to the Old Vic at lunchtime again having spent the morning doing appointments with the kids. When you have a performance looming, the nerves sit beneath everything you have to do in the day, waiting for release. It's what always happens when I'm acting on stage. Took me a bit by surprise as I'm on the other side of things for this.

The second half is more eclectic than the first. Art Malik plays a doctor in the 1980s in my piece about my dad, Jade Anouka plays a young nurse in the 1990s as written by Courttia Newland, Ruth Madeley talks about life in a wheelchair in a piece penned by Matilda Ibini for the 2000s while Louise English sings Seiriol Davies' musical monologue about the NHS now. Gloria sings in between decades again. The dress goes well but it is such a diverse and slightly crazy evening of performance I am unsure how it will be received.

In the break between dress and show, Adrian and I go to see *Seawall* – Andrew Scott in a half-hour monologue by Simon Stephens – which is currently playing in the theatre. It's beautifully performed and written but strange to watch when I have all the NHS voices in my head.

As the audience came in for our show, I get more and more nervous as various friends and associates from the business turn up to watch.

I had completely forgotten that I am a writer tonight. Art plays it well but misses some lines and gets them in the wrong order. That brings the evening sharply into focus and reminds me it was my piece. Nerves and exposure. It goes well, I think, although it is a less polished evening than last night. Drinks in the bar after.

It's such an extraordinary line-up of talent on stage and off and I feel very responsible for them being here and having a good experience. Crazy, really. I won't be able to process this until it's done.

You expose yourself to failure and criticism when you do something new. These actors and writers, Adrian, the Old Vic have worked so hard to make this happen. I hope they all feel it has been worth it.

Friday 29 June

Lolita   8.00 am. I'm writing *Pi* today.

Read over my draft and tweak it. It is almost ready and I am tempted to just send it to producer Simon and Max, but don't. I am always impatient to move forward, always have been, but there's no harm in waiting a bit. It is the right decision.

Adrian   2.00 pm. About to go into the theatre to prep the cast to play both halves of the play/show/evening. Don't want to give them loads of notes. Just want them to work on strengthening what they got out of the shows on Monday and Tuesday.

This will be the first time the full company meet and see each other perform.

I hope nothing goes wrong . . .

5.30 pm. Ok, so I'm sitting in the bar having rehearsed the show through with the cast. Gone cue to cue on all the changes and replotted a few lights and scene changes. Waiting for family members and friends to turn up to watch. This is now completely out of my hands. A strange and very opposing feeling when I think about work in the theatre. Normally, as an actor, the theatre is the place where the work belongs entirely to you. Every beat and moment is controlled by you and your ability to read the other actors and the reactions of the audience. Even their silence has a thousand different qualities in it. Actors will sometimes go back to doing theatre as a way of getting their 'mojo' back. A way to feel that immediate connection and ability to control circumstance that is lost when doing film or television.

So it's weird to be in the theatre for a show I'm completely involved in, and yet have absolutely no control over.

Still, it's the first time I've directed a play or any kind of professional performance. I'll just have to get used to it.

Lolita   5.30 pm. As I drive my youngest daughter and myself to the Old Vic for the final performance of *The Greatest Wealth*, an idea pops into my head of how to end *Pi*. It's a simple bookend: when Okamoto and Lulu come in at the beginning, Pi is not to be seen. He eventually emerges from under his hospital bed and comes out as soon as he knows he has visitors. I think at the very end, when Okamoto and Lulu leave, he should get the biscuits and banana he has hoarded under his sheet and return to his place under the bed. Blackout. Then we'll be left wondering is he Richard Parker or just a traumatized boy? It will mirror the actions of the tiger who takes his food under the tarpaulin of the lifeboat.

10.00 pm. Everyone is at the theatre tonight – family, friends, work colleagues. It is busy and pretty full. My dad is also there. It is lovely for me to have him there – to salute him, his life, his work and his story.

When Art says his name on the stage – 'my name is Bidhan' – it really pleases me. It's my dad's name. He also names my dad's brothers, my uncles. Feels good to mark them all in this grand space.

The show goes well. The audience are appreciative. The cast do a brilliant job and really go for it. A few calls for a prompt but all met with good humour. The audience are somehow let in on the truth of the pretence of theatre, glimpsing the actor behind the character. My dad meets Art Malik afterwards. It is nice to see my dad's reaction.

Stayed for a drink after and got to bed at 2.00 am.

The Old Vic have been very supportive producers. I have learnt so much about other people on this project – the Deaf creative community, the disabled creative community. Through this work I have genuinely stepped inside the perspectives of others. That's the point of theatre, really. So I feel I have honoured my dad and the NHS.

On to the next.

Saturday 30 June

Adrian I didn't get used to it at all. Not in the slightest. It was very strange. Lolita and I sat together unable to keep still. Every time a sentence or a piece of action came across and went down well with the audience we breathed a stifled sigh of relief. Then, there was an interval and before we knew it, the show was over. The actors did a great job. I was surprised by their expertise. The audience reaction was very enthusiastic. People stood up. Many people were in tears, feeling joy at the work the individuals within the health service provide, and anger at the way the NHS has been treated. For many it was anger at the way the NHS had treated the people who work tirelessly to keep it standing.

Everything I wanted us to remember and applaud from this 'celebration' had been realized. An incredible amount of empathy is laced into these pieces, pushing the buttons on our own empathic responses. No one accesses the NHS until they feel very vulnerable or are in pain. It is at this point that we seek the help of doctors and nurses and so the writers, in expressing what the service means to them, have automatically recreated that vulnerability on stage, whether it be in direct address or a speech made as part of a scene.

Courttia Newland's piece about a nurse who is in distress because an older colleague to whom she owes everything is in hospital on palliative care, speaks of duty and love while upsetting the audience with its depiction of a nurse who is at a loss. The nurse, brilliantly played by Jade Anouka, has no idea how to process her friend's approaching death and so fills the air with words. Speaking to people afterward, they said they found the piece upsetting because a nurse is always the one who comforts ... it was jarring to see a nurse in desperate need of a kind word and some reassurance, which Courttia made sure never came. Each piece worked a similar kind of alchemy. The Old Vic was loud with conversation afterwards. Very grateful to Lolita for suggesting me as director for this and to the Old Vic for agreeing. It's been a fascinating project to be a part of.

Spent the day attending the school summer fair with my youngest, her best mate, and best mate's mum and dad. We chatted over burgers and hot dogs about the way education is changing and which teachers are staying or leaving the school.

Sunday 1 July

Lolita   We are supporting a charitable event at Coworth Park. This is one we go to regularly because it helps some excellent causes and is always fun. It is supported by Prince Harry and Prince William.

Beverley Knight is the live act. She is amazing. Her voice is stunning and she's such a consummate performer. It is a good day and raises a lot of money for charity.

Adrian   Met up with Kelly Adams and Robert Glenister from the *Hustle* team at the charity event. Great weather, great company and Beverly Knight performing in the evening was the icing on the cake. I got quite proud of hearing her Birmingham accent when she spoke to us in between songs. The woman has an incredible voice.

Tuesday 3 July

Lolita   I hand in my new draft of *Pi*.

I've tightened the story and made the character journeys have more impact. It reads like a more fluid story now, whereas before it was endless sketchy snapshots. Max's notes from the workshop were great. So the draft has gone.

I find out today that the slot that came up at the RSC is no longer available. They still want *Pi*, but in 2021. That feels too far away. I've been in email contact with Simon who is in the US, opening another show. We'll meet next week with Max to discuss the next stage. We're getting closer to venues, though.

I am disappointed about the RSC but it may be a silver lining. If we had got the slot next year, Max would have been directing another show at the same time so it could have meant a very complicated rehearsal structure.

I also get other disappointing writing news.

A project called *Rolling Over*, which I've been working on for the last twenty years, is rejected again. I wrote a film of it years ago. Then I reinvented it into a three-part, very in-depth TV proposal that charts a true murder story that my dad was involved in 1960. It was a trial that went to the Old Bailey and ended up as front-page news.

I have one more avenue to hear from with this project and then I will have to put it away. Feel disappointed.

In the evening I meet Adrian at the National Theatre to see *The Octaroon*. I'd missed it when it was at The Orange Tree. It has a brilliant opening speech – really engaging, clever, funny. The play itself is crazy and has some fantastically poignant moments that make me look at theatre a little differently. The cast are very good indeed.

Adrian   An incredible evening watching *The Octoroon* in the theatre. Provocative, funny, very dark humour and shot through with a malevolent eye on race in America today.

Branden Jacobs-Jenkins has done something remarkable. He hammers home the racial stereotypes prevalent in Boucicault's play while all the time showing the reality of the time these stereotypes were formed. A time when one race completely dominated all others with laws and social rules that were enforceable by death, and then created alternative facts and fiction in which that domination was justified. 'Facts' that are toxic and still exist today. Much to talk about on the way home.

Wednesday 4 July

Lolita I start to look at the French play *Politically Correct* and see how I am going to tackle that. I've been asked to adapt it for the British stage. This is a play about a man who holds right-wing views meeting a left-wing woman. It asks whether people of opposing political views can have a relationship. It is set against the backdrop of an election in France where the right wing might win.

It's an interesting premise but needs a lot of work in order to make it relevant for a British audience. It could be particularly potent given the swing to the right we are experiencing at this moment.

This adaptation is a different process again to what I've done before. The play has a lot of scenes so I go through it, marking out the dramatic moments, and filtering it down this way.

I begin to research right- and left-wing politics. As I read about them, I notice how the language shifts between both sides and how although they share the same words, it is with entirely different intent. For example, they may talk about 'freedom' but it means very different things for each side. I start to get ideas.

The argument between right and left is so insidious and ugly in real life that I want to capture the grey area in my version, where you might switch allegiance because they both make sense. It's what I did with Pierre and Ira in *Red Velvet*: it isn't clear-cut. Nothing ever is.

I try to learn my lines for *Riviera*. They're going in slowly. Not that I have many of them, but it's just a different muscle.

Friday 6 July

Adrian Got invited to see Lenny Henry's sixtieth birthday show at BBC studios, Wood Lane. I am kind of in awe of this man. Now just hoping the ever-changing *Rook* schedule might allow me the time to get there. Just have to wait and see.

Tuesday 10 July

Lolita   I am in Nice. I got here yesterday. I'm filming.

I'm finding it hard to focus. I had notes from Leo on my story plan for *Invisible Cities*.

I have been planning to take August off from writing, so I need to get on with Leo's notes now. The notes are good, the story is big, and I have three weeks in which to do a loose first draft.

But I am filming *Riviera* and although my part is limited, it still requires attention. I've learnt my lines and need to be present for this.

I am also pre-planning *Politically Correct*, reading up on right-wing ideology and trying to work out how I will make this a piece that discusses political beliefs a personal story you want to follow. Can't focus clearly on that either.

I have agreed to speak at the graduation ceremony at RADA on Saturday. I'm the graduate speaker at the end of it all so need to say something useful and interesting. I am trawling my memories and thoughts and trying to make them into a coherent ten-minute speech.

I am also trying to book a family holiday and don't know whether Adrian can come because of his filming schedule, which is never released much in advance. I need to find a possibility for all of us so I can move quickly when we know his schedule.

The internet supposedly makes life easier, but the flights I look at seem to be an illusion; as soon as I decide and try to book them, they are removed from the options. Frustrating to say the least.

Ok, time to be an actor. I play an art curator for the Clios family – make-up, costume, action!

Wednesday 11 July

Lolita   I am on the plane flying back from Nice. Feeling very reflective.

I filmed yesterday. It was fine. It was in a studio where they filmed *Les Enfants du paradis*. They'd built an old stone art gallery in there with key pieces of art on display that my character had curated. It was impressive. The attention to detail in TV when they have money available makes for impressive work.

I was in one scene where I didn't speak and then had a few lines in another scene. It was fine but I was aware that I was just adding colour to the story for the main character. It's hard to switch off my writing head when I act. I dissect scenes and what each character serves.

In the evening I did some notes in readiness for writing today. I made my notes whilst having the World Cup on TV. I'm not a football fan but have watched some of the World Cup this year because my youngest daughter has really got into it so has inspired me too. England are doing so well. Semi-final tonight.

Last night was France v. Belgium and France won. The car horns and the cheering in the streets went on for hours. Jasmine texted from her school trip in Kent saying that France had won. Sat in my hotel room in Nice, I texted that I could hear the celebrations. Lila texted from her holiday in Spain and Adrian from Birmingham!

So today, feeling slightly nervous, I embark on my first draft of *Invisible Cities*. A daunting prospect. But I've done some good prep and notes so I follow the map of what I set out before. I always find a first draft hard. I walk away often and then write in short sharp bursts.

The plane is delayed by half an hour for take-off, so I do some work in that gap. Whether it is good or not, who knows.

Thursday 12 July

Adrian An unexpected day away from shooting. Among other things I try to get busy with the idea of finding a space for training. I went out to put my name down with various estate agents on the local high street. It may be futile, but I want to find the Taekwondo classes a permanent home. I'm looking forward to the day we can invite different practitioners over to one building in south-east London to share their knowledge of other styles and the street fighting or competition fighting effectiveness of their techniques. Perhaps I have to walk this path a little to find out just how expensive and unworkable this idea is.

Friday 13 July

Lolita   I'm climbing uphill a little. School holidays are on and while I love that lack of structure, not having to get up at 6.30 am and see them off to school, you also suffer from it.

I am squeezing writing into any gaps I can find while trying not to compromise the quality of my family time. Impossible? Square peg, round hole?

Writing *Invisible Cities* is hard but exhilarating. I am taking Leo's note of 'write the impossible and they will make it happen'. Okay then. I am writing opium-fuelled visions of floating into clouds where cities exist above the audience.

Have a meeting this morning with Max and Simon about *Pi*. Now the RSC is off the table (although their offer of 2021 still stands but feels too distant), we are aiming for a co-production with other theatres.

We'll find out next week which ones but it looks like this would all kick off with rehearsals in March. I am struck by this timing. The kids have significant birthdays in March (all birthdays are significant, of course) but in June, when we'd be playing at a theatre, I'll turn fifty.

Simon and Max start to talk about the next stage for the script. I am not quite ready for that and felt slightly sick. Can I do all this work? It all happens next year. *Invisible Cities* will be in July with rehearsals in May and June. What about my acting? What about *Red Velvet* and *Politically Correct*?

Too many questions. Best to do an hour on *Invisible Cities* and then step down for a much-needed weekend.

Saturday 14 July

Lolita   I always try to take weekends off but my head is so full of open projects I feel like it's pushing me to work. I resist. You have to recharge or the thoughts won't come. I am quite bloody-minded about my weekends: I only write if there's no other choice. The problem is that I can't settle to do something leisurely. I'd love to read a novel but my head has no space, so I wander about the house resisting work and doing chores. There is a simplicity in household chores that I have learned to enjoy. They don't require too much thought and they get achieved – a simple equation of work equals results.

This afternoon I go to RADA to speak at this year's graduation ceremony. It is very nice – informal but formal. On the Jerwood stage (aka the Vanbrugh), Ken Branagh, who is RADA's president, presents an honorary fellowship to Thelma Holt. Ed Kemp, RADA's principal, and Stephen Waley-Cohen, RADA's chairman of the board, give speeches. Eighty students receive their certificates and then it's my turn to speak.

I have been thinking about this all week. I ran through options in my hotel room in Nice, talking it out to myself, and trying it on. I felt the need to say something meaningful but that felt very pressured. How can you say something that matters? So I take that pressure off myself and just speak about my experiences at RADA and how they underpin all my work.

It is a pleasure to go back there as I progress through the industry because it reminds me how I started. I am very struck by the changing tide of the business. Thelma Holt is in her eighties and trained here. Thelma speaks of there being far fewer women in her year because the business didn't need them. Unthinkable now. And as to people of colour – I didn't ask. A world apart in the same room.

It is a lovely event, the students are shining and their families are there. Now I see what a collection of forces facilitates things in your life. We very rarely, if ever, do anything alone.

Thursday 19 July

Lolita   I have been in Nice since Monday filming *Riviera*. I go home today.

It has been a week of long days of filming with not much to do, which is always more tiring. I was in the background on Tuesday and on Wednesday I was in first thing, had hours off in the middle and was filming till 11.30 pm.

The people on this job are very nice and the fact Adrian was a regular in the first series means I get the benefit of his involvement. I do feel like I've entered his class at school. People speak very well of him for both his acting and directing. They are a strong company of actors to work with which makes my being in the background more bearable. Since I have no responsibility other than to deliver the lines I'm given, I choose to be more productive elsewhere . . .

I spend every gap in my dressing room writing *Invisible Cities*. I brought *Pi* and *Politically Correct* here too – in their very different stages.

Pi – I'm trying to think of a way to bring the shipwreck closer to the beginning of the script without spoiling its charm. It becomes a bit overt if you give everything at the start, so I am spending time thinking of moving scenes around like chess pieces without losing the essence of Yann Martel's story.

Politically Correct – as Donald Trump and his idiocies escalate, it is hard to see how to write a piece about left- and right-wing politics without feeling either tub thumping or naive. In the real world, the right wing is gaining ground. The press are reporting more about them and their views are now being welcomed into a legitimate forum. They are part of the conversation when before they were treated with caution. Donald Trump says more and more incendiary statements that facilitate hate. If I base *Politically Correct* now, it will date quickly. I think I'll have to place it a bit in the future and see how I go.

Reminds me of when Adrian did *Primary Colors* – a fantastic film directed by the late, great Mike Nichols – a fictional take on Bill Clinton's 1992 presidential campaign. Adrian played his campaign manager. By the time this beautiful film came out, though, the real news about Clinton and Monica Lewinsky and impeachment were being picked apart on every media site possible. As a result, the film didn't stand up to what was genuinely happening at the time and didn't do as well as expected.

I have to think of a way of talking about the right and left that is timeless and not linked to what is happening now but that links to a cycle of right-wing leanings in history. Hmmm.

Anyway, off to catch my plane home and more *Invisible Cities* while I do that.

Adrian   Had a ninety-minute conference call with producers Jeffery and Luke to go over Jeffrey's notes on my latest version of *Lottery Boy*. Over the phone we basically did a page-turn full of detailed commentary. It was a necessary process, showing me the kind of film both men think I have written. We surprised each other. They completely missed things I had put into the script and thought were clear, while at the same time, they picked up on things that were obvious to them but that I had no idea I had let slip into the story.

After the call, I felt buoyed by their obvious commitment and the doors Jeffrey's involvement has brought us to. But I also now feel daunted by the amount of work I've put on my plate especially as Jeffrey can't really knock on those doors until he has a new draft from me.

Saturday 21 July

Lolita Have come away to a cabin in the New Forest with Lila, my eldest. It's a rare opportunity for the two of us to spend some time together. We have a laugh and cook together. Adrian has gone to Paris with Jasmine, our youngest. It's beautiful here – peaceful and wide. This morning I write *Invisible Cities* and because it's the school holidays I break my usual rules and write whenever I can. I now have a fifty-page script.

The journey from having nothing to where I am now feels immense and yet I've done it in a couple of weeks. What is it about writing that feels so impossible to start?

Anyway Leo sends a big document with many references for the production – design, inspirations, info about Marco Polo and Kublai Khan. I use some of Marco Polo's diary in the play – no one will know but me – but it adds hidden texture I think.

Have a very good chat with Sarah, my acting agent, on Friday. I need to tell her that these two writing projects will take up the middle of next year. If it all works out, which it looks like it might, I will be off the acting circuit from 25 March to the end of July 2019. If I am able to have my cake and eat it, I expressed a desire to do some substantial filming before then. It doesn't have to be a major part, a good guest or something, but something that requires some actual acting. I'd like to stretch those muscles a bit before I go into writer mode.

Sarah is great. She's not fazed at all by my writing. I like that.

A few years back, a friend, also in the industry, told me not to talk about my writing whilst auditioning for acting jobs. She said people would feel uncomfortable that I did both. I have since realized that advice was given because *she* felt uncomfortable about me doing both. I find it difficult not to talk about both sides of my work because they are both very public. I also realized that most people know I write anyway. If you deny half of yourself in the room, then you only show half of your abilities.

It was a good lesson for me: when some people give you advice, it is more often about their limitations and not yours.

Sunday 22 July

Adrian   Took a weekend break to Paris with my youngest. Get some air . . . see some sights, go to the Louvre. On my way back from Paris to London. while waiting to board the train, I went into the bathroom. A cleaner coming out of the ladies loos took one look at me and said, 'Eh . . . vous! C'est vous! Huh?!'

She was quite loud. It took me a little by surprise and alerted other passengers sitting within earshot that something was wrong. I tried to be polite. ' Pardon Madame, je ne sais pas ce que vous voul . . .'. She cut me off. 'Non . . . c'est vous!'

Someone exiting the female bathroom had now stopped and was looking at me. I had already guessed what was coming and continued on into the men's toilet, hoping she may be busy doing something else when I came out. No such luck.

When I came out of the bathroom, a gendarme stepped into my path and stood looking at me; bystanders were looking at the two of us. People out of earshot had no idea what was going on but were beginning to stare at me being stopped by an officer. Outside the loo.

'Are you an actor?', he asked, with a heavy Parisian accent, smiling at me. 'Yes, I am,' I replied, kind of wanting the floor to open up.

'Ah . . .,' he said, nodding. 'She thought so.' He indicates the cleaner, who is beaming and pointing at my face. She hands the gendarme a phone.

'She would like to take picture?'

'Yes,' I say. 'Er, but perhaps . . . pas dans la salle de bain?' I smile and he laughs a little, but she is stony-faced, as if I've reprimanded her.

'Ok, ok . . .,' she says, taking my arm and leading me out into the waiting area, destroying any hope I had that this could possibly be discreet.

I put my arm around her and smile. Y'know, as you do. All I need now is for her flash to be on so that more people look, recognize me and start to take photos of me having a photo taken (trust me, this has happened).

Anyway, the gendarme takes the picture. No flash. She has one look and is pleased. Well done, Mr Gendarme. Man obviously knows how to point and shoot . . . (sorry).

I go back and join Jasmine who is smiling at me. She knows it was kind of public and not the sort of thing I would normally agree to at all. I am quite firm when I'm with the kids. I don't want them standing around while a picture is taken. Don't know why. I just want that part of the job to be put to one side. I always politely say no so that when I'm with them, I'm with them. But . . . I don't know, this gendarme . . . maybe it was his smile, maybe I'm a sucker for a man in uniform, maybe it was the gun on his hip.

Monday 23 July

Adrian Have to do a taping today for a film role. They had sent the lines to me on Friday evening, gave me a deadline to record the scenes and get it back to them in the US by Monday afternoon. They never send scripts any more, but just throw a net out to have any actor who may look right put themselves on tape so that they can show it to the director for interest.

Best get to it. I start to set up the iPad and phone to read and record. I used to advise actors to learn their lines. I still believe it's important to have most of what you need to say learned and in your head so you can play with the responses. But it's always good to have the lines off screen handy too, so that you can eliminate a tension that comes from 'trying' to remember what you have to say next.

About ten years ago, I received a couple of pages from a UK casting director (who shall remain nameless). The scene was a male character having a phone conversation. It was about a page and a half of dialogue where the person on the other end of the line interrupted the character constantly so that their reactions went from reasonable to very angry. I thought it was worth some effort because not only would it be a nice line of emotion to play, it was also supposed to be for an untitled Marvel project. I pushed things to one side and focused on trying to get the lines learned.

It would need some work. The lines were lots of disjointed thoughts being fired off at speed. I was shooting something else at the time so it took me a few days going back and forth with the words finding a meaning and learning it so that it could be delivered at a good pace.

When I finally went in for the meeting, I chatted to the casting director for a little while before we set about recording the scene. She was going to read with me.

She put the camera on and I started. It was going ok, then about ten seconds in she forgot to give me the line, I didn't want to make it up or pretend (because it wouldn't have made any sense) so I stopped.

'Sorry,' I said, 'but I think . . .' 'Oh, I'm so sorry,' she apologized. 'Let's go again.'

So she restarts the camera and off I go. I've spent hours on this and want to get it right.

Sure enough, after a few moments of dialogue, she trips up and gives me the wrong cue and then stops talking. Again, I stop. I'm stuck if she doesn't read the lines in the right order because the scene needs to build so that I can do my job by showing a little of what I could do if the part – the unnamed untitled part – were given to me. She has the lines on her lap.

She apologizes again and then tells me that it doesn't really matter about the lines being in the right order.

I humbly explain that I've learned them and they won't make sense if . . . She interrupts me and explains with a tight smile that the project is 'untitled'. I stop speaking and stare at her, puzzled. She explains, politely that these lines are from a different movie just being sent out to you to, you know, see what actors are around. They just want to hear your American accent and see your face.

I know I'm getting angry. I don't want to, but I can feel it.

'What?' I ask, as politely as I can. 'Then why not just tape me chatting to you in the accent? Why put me to all this trouble?' I think that was a little too direct. There's a moment of silence as she most likely comes to the conclusion that she has one of those 'difficult' actors sitting across from her.

I try to placate.

'I've just spent a while learning it and trying to look different.' I sheepishly indicate my jacket, shirt and tie. She gently puts the script to one side and we slowly manage to chat about other things. She never turns the camera back on, but smiles and tells me that she has enough material to send them. As I leave, I know that tape is never going to leave her office.

It's only in hindsight that I realize I have been in to see that casting director only one other time in the ten years since that audition. Something about that meeting is unresolved for me. It sits in my memory as some kind of reminder, but I'm not sure of what.

Anyway. I look at the pages I now have in front of me. They have sent four scenes that the character is in. Two of them require me to move or grab hold of another character, there's some other physical action required so I choose only one scene that shows the character dealing with a kind of repressed despair. I record myself on an iPhone with Lolita off screen, reading in the other lines.

A few years ago I bought a set of lights, a digital camera, an external microphone and a large chroma key grey back cloth. It was the kind of set-up you find at Spotlight or any casting directors office. I would spend hours setting the equipment up, recording myself for films or TV projects and then taking the equipment down before sitting in front of my computer to edit the material. Since then, the Apple and Android phones have been developed so much that the video quality is the same as the digital camera I had bought four years before. So now, when I record difficult dialogue, I place my iPad on a music stand angled toward me so that the lines are scrolling in my peripheral vision, while my phone is set up on an octopus tripod connected to the music stand. I place myself against a wall facing bay windows with net curtains so that the light covers a wide area and is diffused. I have reflectors ready if I need to create a different mood or bounce the light in a different direction and off I go. Once the scene is recorded, I put it straight into my laptop so that I can add my own title and end cards with my name, the project, my agent and the character I'm going for, before I upload the completed take to my agent.

I prefer auditioning in this way. It means I can do as many takes as I like, watch each one back and change performance as necessary. Still takes a few hours, though.

Wednesday 25 July

Lolita   I finish my first draft of *Invisible Cities*.

I've been working every spare moment I have because in the school holidays (and with an ongoing acting job abroad) it is hard to get the hours clear to do it. Consequently I have written on trains, planes, airport lounges, my Winnebago, hotel rooms, everywhere but my office. I have a bit of an ache in my neck from all the awkward places I have been writing but it is done (for now). I am pleased with it.

I have translated the book into a fifty-page two-hander. I've managed to answer a lot of questions with this first draft: where people are, how they speak, what motivates them, what is the problem they are looking to solve and how it is dealt with. The novel has no narrative at all, just image after image with a backdrop of smoking opium which means anything can happen. In imagining all the elements of digital projection, the use of water, dance, music and language, I feel pleased to have found a narrative arc.

Anyway the best bit of all is finishing and reaching a plateau where you can rest for a moment. I send it to the producers at MIF, Leo and his team at 59, my literary agent Katie, Tina and Adrian.

In the evening we go to the Royal Academy summer art show with friends. They are artists and have work displayed there. We then have dinner in the RA club. It is a fascinating night peppered with stories of eminent artists. There is a lot of laughing.

It is good to hear other straight-talkers. I often find that at the high end of artistic appreciation, there are a lot of 'educated' people who can make you feel like you don't know enough to join in, when the truth of it is every one of us has enough education to have a valid opinion – how you respond is how you respond.

Adrian   Sara Shamma and her husband Mounzer have invited us to the Royal Academy to have a look at the summer show with David Mach and Lyndsey Gibb. We spend a good few hours going around the Academy looking at the art on display. Normally I find walking around galleries an interesting but very passive exercise, but this is great. It's illuminated by being in the presence of such great artists who bring their expertise and knowledge to the discussions about each piece.

Smaller pieces tucked away in a corner are brilliant examples of the artists' patience and skill followed by other artists (some of whom are quite famous) who've spent little to no time preparing their piece. They know they're selling their name, nothing more.

Afterwards we chat animatedly through mouthfuls of food about the nature of art and the mechanics of generating an emotional response in a passive viewer.

We end the evening talking about south London, the Horniman Museum, Dulwich Picture Gallery, and how great it would be to have a connection between all the arts venues in the area. Perhaps an arts festival of sorts that could include live performances and sculpture? It can seem as though nothing travels further south than the South Bank. Mounzer chats about a studio space for painters and I mention the need for a space to house the Taekwondo classes in a permanent home. I know it's a bit of a reach, but it's an art form in itself, albeit from a completely different perspective.

By the time we're on our way home, I'm tipsy and certain we're about to take over Southwark and Lewisham councils.

Thursday 26 July

Adrian   Cycled over to have a look at the Ambassadors Theatre with Simon and James. We have a firm offer to use it for *Cyrano* from mid-February next year.

It's a lovely space tucked away at the top of St Martin's Lane. It's also a very small venue: just the place if you want to perform a play that communicates its ideas mainly through language and plot. We all agree that it's not the kind of space that can contain the physical romp of huge emotions and images that we want our *Cyrano* to be. The Garrick Theatre is still a possibility. All three of us want that to work. Nica Burns is juggling a few things and can't tell us yet, but we are waiting, holding our breath. Let's see. There has been some reluctance for other spaces to commit as the play has been spoken about with various actors in the lead role from a few theatres. Once they have had a conversation with one actor it would be bad practice for them to jump onto another version with me in the lead. They are also aware that whomever does the play first will cancel the idea for the other theatres. Added to this there is apparently a British actor, who has been working in Hollywood for a long while, who has been talking about doing the play with a West End producer. A greater movie profile means better box office which in turn means a West End opening with no need to try the play out of town first. This is the area that has tripped us up with our version. I don't know who the actor is but I can see that it's a profile I don't have. Some spaces want to wait and see what happens to these other conversations before committing to me in the role.

We have some good possibilities outside London, but nothing suitable in the city yet. I will hold my breath. Mike has done a great translation and Simon Evans is a great director; maybe this will still work.

Saturday 28 July

Lolita   I am about to stop writing on 1 August. I remember in 2012 when *Red Velvet* (the play) was finally produced I thought that if I don't work very hard at my writing for the next couple of years, *Red Velvet* would be a one-off.

I chose to work.

Here I am six years later – finally having a break. Every family holiday I have taken since *Red Velvet* was produced (one week a year, as that's all we ever manage to coordinate between us), bar the holiday after my mum passed away, I have written, researched and worked. Last year I was learning my lines for *Hamlet*. I have been productive and have many scripts to show for all those years, but none of them have been produced. (Yet. Adrian keeps reminding me of that.)

I have six scripts all in varying stages. I have pitched many ideas, done extensive treatments and story arcs for two original TV series. It's been a lot of work with no fulfilment at the end. It's good to stop sometimes and look at the results rather than just charging on.

The great thing about acting is you get hired and you do it.

I cannot wait for August to come along. I have work meetings but no writing. At all. I want to read novels. I am unable to read while I write because all of my headspace is consumed by my research, the stories in my head and any lines I need to learn for acting.

I think what I'm looking forward to most this August is to having a free and literally open mind. To think thoughts without dwelling constantly on solving the problems in a script. To read and get lost in someone else's version of the world, someone else's story. To watch TV and films and theatre and escape again.

Monday 30 July

Adrian I'm trying to get my fiftieth birthday free from *The Rook* production. I checked the dates with them about six weeks ago, at which point they said they would try but because the episodes hadn't been written yet they couldn't give me official clearance. I've asked if I can go away with the family to celebrate (commiserate) my fiftieth and my father-in-law's eighty-fifth (as our birthdays are a day apart) at the same time. It's that one week of the year we try to fit in a family holiday.

I've waited for a month only to see that the latest schedule shows me filming right through the days I booked to be clear. I check the dates against the scenes being shot and the locations needed and can see that this is completely avoidable. I'm going to have to make a few phone calls.

Tuesday 31 July

Lolita I have a meeting with Hedda and Marilyn from Fiery Angel this morning about *Politically Correct*. The premise is interesting but given what is going on in the world now and this horrible leaning to the right across Europe and the US, it's nowhere near provocative enough.

I've spent some time deconstructing the original play. There are nineteen scenes and in between the scenes there is a constant news feed about a right-wing party on the cusp of winning elections. I want to bring the outside world into the play differently. I have an idea of getting one actor to play all the key players in the political world of the play. I think it would be fun for the actor but also for the audience, and very theatrical.

Anyway, I tell Hedda and Marilyn my ideas and they like them. I hadn't realized how much work I'd done, actually. When you pose a question in your head, your subconscious keeps analysing it and trying to find an answer when you might think you have moved on.

That's what is really good about leaving drafts to ferment, to brew, to reveal themselves later. I can feel that I'm learning to be a better writer. Learning to say what I mean more succinctly.

The meeting goes well but now I have to write it. It's one thing to have the ideas but quite another to deliver them. I can't get to this till November, so plenty of time to mull.

I spend the afternoon at home working on reordering the first half of *Pi*, so we get to the shipwreck quicker. It's thrown the story up in the air and I find myself moving between the hospital and the ship more frequently. Max said fewer scenes are better but if we want the boat sooner then we'll have to move about more. Anyway, I follow the story. It will show me the way. I find this forward and backward movement through narrative a bit like kneading bread. It feels like you're getting nowhere but actually the texture is becoming richer.

It's the end of the day and I am a little frustrated when I have to stop as I haven't completed the task. I know I don't have enough time to reshape the first half – I have only had a couple of days. Still I am determined to turn the computer off. That's it. No more writing till September.

I check my email chain before I do and see that Hedda and Marilyn have asked me for a single-page pitch of my version of *Politically Correct*. I was going to leave it for a few weeks but it's only a page. I open up a document and begin writing it.

Later that evening I watch a beautifully crafted episode of *The Handmaid's Tale*. It is great to watch excellence. Makes you up your game.

Wednesday 1 August

Lolita   This afternoon I go to 59 Production offices for the design-concept meeting of *Invisible Cities*. Director Leo and his colleague Jenny present their thoughts to the producers and production staff connected with MIF, the CEO and AD of Rambert and me. The designs are ambitious and big. It is all displayed on a large screen showing drawings and ideas of the venues with key elements they want to explore. It looks enormous and impressive. The MIF production team start asking about logistics and what materials they could use.

Because 59 are presenting these designs before most people in the room have read the script, I am wondering how my role will develop. They are talking about elements they want to see without referring to any story. Will I now be required to write to order? Do I have to follow the development of design first, rather than leading with story?

Speaking to Leo and Jenny afterwards, I get the impression that they want to remain collaborative within the restrictions of what Leo's vision needs. If water needs to emerge slowly through the performance, then that needs to be incorporated into how I tell the story.

We make a date in early September to meet and discuss.

The artistic director of MIF asks me if I have ideas for casting. I suggest four actors of whom three are black and one is Japanese. He says we should cast to the correct race as there has been a big story around Robert Lepage who has cancelled a show he directed about slavery in which not one member of the cast was of colour. Of course Lepage's casting was wrong, but is the solution for other productions to make sure everyone only plays the race they appear to be?

I have always believed there should be diversity in performance. Actors should be allowed to play anything. Of course this is the exact same argument that narrow-minded practitioners have used to keep mainstream casting white. It is difficult therefore to use this argument to push for greater diversity when the words seem to restrict and reduce the opportunities of others.

In the future, I hope anyone will be allowed to play anything but in order to get there, first we have to deconstruct the mess we are in.

Friday 3 August

Adrian Spent this last week shooting *The Rook* every day. The heatwave is sapping the energy out of us all. Why did I think it would be a good idea to have this character wear three-piece suits? It's the suit-wearing, posh-accent type of character that has been coming my way ever since I played Mickey Bricks for seven years in *Hustle*. I know it works and I also know that a lot of people have great difficulty seeing me as anything else. So, here I am, sweating while desperately trying to look cool in a bespoke three-piece suit.

The family have all booked to go away for a week's holiday. We don't know whether I'll be able to join them. Had an amended shooting schedule sent through for *The Rook*. The dates are looking better. It's not completely sorted, but it's better. As things stand now, they'll all have to go without me.

Saturday 4 August

Adrian   I'm staring at my notes for *Lottery Boy* knowing I have to give Luke and Jeffrey a pretty good draft of the film by the end of September. Jeffrey has some people he wants to take the script to in London and everyone seems to be waiting for me to turn out a great new draft. I just want to get on with creating the images and situations through the lens but I'm being held back by the job of writing, which is a skill I am no master of. My act of writing this script was simply to clean the book of any story that would not translate to the screen and then create the links necessary to build what was left into a believable story. But with this set of notes on tone, the certificate we want, the actors we need to get on board before we get the budget and therefore rewriting the roles so that they become more attractive, it's all starting to feel very difficult. This is the world I have watched Lolita work in for years. Frustrated by the lack of roles for an actress like her, she started writing. She worked hard and did a lot of practice, short story by short story, until she began to share ideas for series, films and plays. She got asked to write treatments and breakdowns and pitch documents all for nothing. Then she gets feedback from people asking her to change them. That's a lot of time spent jumping through the hoops of everyone's notes without any payment or guarantee of a green light at the end of it. Years spent writing on spec. Now here I am with my first effort getting a taste of what she often goes through.

I've been offered a directing gig on a teaser for the pilot of a new comedy drama. It isn't green-lit yet. The company want to use the teaser to try and get the series sold to a channel. Good people are involved. I don't want it to detract from work on *Lottery Boy* in the autumn or the possibility of *Cyrano* needing to rehearse before the end of the year depending on what theatre we get. The concrete offer in hand is not as dear to me as the possibilities I've set in motion.

Monday 6 August

Lolita   So *Pi* – the dates have gone awry. We were waiting to hear of an offer from a London theatre but the dates have changed and they have offered a slot that doesn't line up with the offer from another theatre. So now, again, we wait.

All this practice at waiting and I'm not getting any better at it.

My second play, *Calmer*, which I began writing four years ago, got stuck at a theatre that was indecisive about it. After over three years at that theatre, I retrieved it from them and have sent it out to other theatres. Again, I have to wait.

Calmer is a contemporary play about three generations of women in the same family. I am looking at the pressure women are under to achieve everything – motherhood, marriage, career – and all the time, we try to make it look effortless. In it I explore the inordinate pressure placed on young women/girls from social media, general media and the judgement of their mothers. It makes for a powder keg of expectations and failure.

The play is also about narcissism and toxicity. My generation is spectator to the rise of the selfie. The obsession with self. The preoccupation with body, diet, achieving, selling your successful life so that people will like you.

The narcissist will do whatever it takes to elevate themselves at the cost of everyone around them. No one is safe. It is a vitriolic, ugly, spiteful state of mind that the narcissist justifies by lying in order to make themselves the victim or hero of a self-created story. I have been studying narcissism for some time now.

I am desperate to see this play fulfilled. But I have to wait.

Tuesday 7 August

Lolita   I see my friend Rosa Maggiora for lunch at London Bridge. We talk about a couple of shows she's designing and all of my various projects. Always nice to catch up with her. We produced a short film together a few years back, *Of Mary*, and Adrian directed it. It did well on the short film festival circuit. It spurred us on to produce a feature that I wrote called *For Joy*. This is based on a monologue I wrote for the Almeida about a woman who suffers a mental breakdown and loses her kid. But we could not get production funding. We got development money from the BFI but then stalled. It was so frustrating because I really enjoy working with her. So we closed our company and have put the film to rest for the time being.

I have now pitched a different idea to the Roundhouse that would involve us working together, so fingers crossed we get to do that.

Simon rang me about *Pi*. He's had a conversation with Sheffield Crucible and they are still keen to have it, which is great news. We would preview for ten or more performances and then open in our last week. Sheffield has a great reputation and that makes me feel better after the challenges of last week. Simon is also going back to the other London venue to see if they will move their dates back. If they don't, we'll do Sheffield. It would also free up some money to do a two-week workshop in December – so it's all good. We should have an answer imminently.

If we do Sheffield, it will be a bit mad because *Invisible Cities* will be happening at the same time, so I'd have to work it out. Also if we do Sheffield, I am sure there will be some international interest to be cultivated from MIF.

I get a call from Max about a script meeting he'd had about *Pi* with dramaturg Jack Bradley. We're all going to work together on Friday, so it'll be good to hear their thoughts.

Wednesday 8 August

Lolita   I get a call from Simon regarding *Pi*. Sheffield Crucible would mean we rehearse five weeks in London hopefully from 20 May next year, tech for a week, preview for ten performances and then open up there with a view to come into London if all goes well.

He says that aside from the workshop we have planned in September, he would like to do a further two-week workshop in December and another one in March/April so that the script is really tight.

The dates mean that *Pi* and *Invisible Cities* will rehearse and open at roughly the same time. Exhilarating, scary, logistically challenging but ultimately doable. There is something about Sheffield that feels right. I am very excited.

I know that I am going to have to work incredibly hard when September starts. Two stories needing equal and epic attention at the same time will be challenging. But to actually have dates for productions that are going to happen is thrilling and the biggest motivator of all.

The lack of production on my other projects has been equal parts demoralizing and frustrating. So to stand here now, on the threshold of two shows both going on at the same time is the very definition of being stuck at the station for a few years and then two trains coming along at once.

Adrian An unexpected offer has come through for me to sing Sky Masterson in *Guys and Dolls* at the Royal Albert Hall. Whenever I'm offered the chance to sing at an awards ceremony or a charity gig, I usually take it. The performance gives me a strong excuse to get myself 'in voice' and work all of those pitching and breathing muscles that may have been resting for too long and gotten sloppy.

The last couple of times I've performed a song for any reason I have been extremely disappointed with the result. At one performance, I was completely under confident and lost my nerve at the eleventh hour. My voice came out sounding weak and wavering. On another occasion I made sure my voice was ready but because I couldn't make the day to rehearse with the band onstage, I found myself on stage at the event in front of an audience lost in reverb, unable to discern the absolute pitch and rhythm within the orchestra. I was furious, with no one more than myself.

Guys and Dolls is an old musical. A clean, amusing, boy meets girl type of thing. As far as show-stopping numbers go there are a few, but the only real blast is 'Sit Down, You're Rockin' the Boat'. Clive Rowe will be singing this part. Clive won an Olivier award for singing it at the National Theatre. I saw that performance and remember him bringing the house down with Sharon D. Clark. Clark Peters gave a suave and very smooth Sky Masterson in that show. In this offer, Clive is a big draw for me. The producers, Fiery Angel, put *Red Velvet* into the West End as part of Ken Branagh's season and are lovely people to work for. The other draw for me apart from the other cast involved is that it's at the Royal Albert Hall with the Royal Philharmonic Orchestra. The opportunity to get my voice in gear and sing on that stage is too good to pass up. Then I hear that Sharon D. Clarke will be involved too. It has become a no-brainer. The whole engagement is only really three weeks long. The director Stephen Mears has asked for us to be off book when we start rehearsals as there will be choreography involved. I say yes and ask for a bit more information about the form the performance will take.

Thursday 9 August

Adrian It's been a while since I met with Karen and Deiderick at Kudos, where I pitched them three ideas for new TV series. They liked one of my pitches and before doing a deal with them, Karen wanted to sit with me to talk about how the story would work each week. What central idea, form and character/s would drive the plot forward?

Karen started with Kudos as a script supervisor on our first series of *Hustle*. By the time we were shooting our last series, she was the exec producer. I'm not used to pitching ideas for shows. I'm an actor, so this is new territory for me. I can see that the way I pitched the idea to her and Deiderick was basically me telling them what the first half of the first episode would look and feel like on television. They could see the world of the characters and they liked the form that the series would take. What they were missing was a driving central plotline – an essential story arc that would keep the audience watching and coming back each week.

I needed to go away and have a think.

There is a script that Lolita and I wrote about eighteen years ago that I feel would provide the correct circumstances for the drama. Its central plot would be ideal for the series. I could use it to build the first two episodes as a two-parter to launch all of the characters.

I drop Karen an email and we make a loose date for November. This gives me the chance to get *Guys and Dolls* done and then start work on *Lottery Boy* and my Kudos idea.

Friday 10 August

Lolita I have a meeting with Max and Simon about *Pi*.

It is meant to be a script meeting but more excitingly we talk through the imminent possibility of Sheffield in May next year. We are working out schedules. It is a direct clash with rehearsals for *Invisible Cities*, but if we can rehearse most of *Pi* in London, that would make things easier. Also Sheffield and Manchester are not far from each other, so commuting between the two would be fine.

We talk through creatives and Max wants up to fifteen actors. There is a bit of light negotiating with Simon and we get to thirteen actors with the possibility of two more.

I'm so pleased to be finally moving forward. I've so enjoyed working with Simon. He obviously has the commercial side to consider but is also keen to do the work creative justice. He's also been very up front and included me in much of the decision-making. And he has constantly pushed us to the next stage. A really good producer.

We then have a script meeting on my last draft of *Pi*. They have incorporated thoughts from Jack Bradley and give me his main points as well as their own. Max is great – clear, uncompromising but open. He gives good notes and allows me to understand what he wants without being prescriptive.

I tell them I can rejig the structure of the play loosely before the workshop on 10 September and maybe write a couple of versions of a scene.

We agree a work timetable, a workshop in September, two weeks in December, one week in March and after each of them I will take three weeks to deliver a new draft. Then we'll be ready for rehearsal.

There is much work ahead and I know I have to be fit and clear for it, but there is nothing as exciting as working towards an actual production. It should hopefully be confirmed in the next few days.

Saturday 11 August

Adrian Went to see *Killer Joe* at Trafalgar Studios. It was directed by Simon and produced by James, who I'm working with on *Cyrano*. Orlando Bloom and the cast were very good. It's a dark play. Tracy Letts is no stranger to tackling what is cruel and offensive but setting it in such a clever way that I knew my sensibilities were being manipulated. I didn't know what was worse: the characters saying and doing those things to each other, or that the author thought it would be a good idea for the characters to say and do those things to each other. I leave the theatre with a strong respect for the actors. It was emotional, powerful, twisted stuff. They gave fine performances even though it was their second show of the day.

As I walk across Trafalgar Square making my way to the Strand, it's dark. I'm by Charing Cross station – the area where I've imagined some of the scenes for *Lottery Boy*. I head off into the darker streets away from the station, crouching, taking pictures from various angles with my phone, gutters, stairways, bins, fire escapes. It'll be useful to look at these alongside many of the other shots I've taken while I work on the script.

The family all go off on holiday at 3.00 am. I will be able to join them in two days after a day's shooting, which gives me a five-day holiday this year. We promise ourselves that we have to take more time away together more often. Setting aside five days in a year for us to be together on holiday is not enough.

Monday 13 August

Lolita   We are in Cyprus for a family holiday. We are in a villa near Deftera, where it is baking hot, beautiful and the opposite of London life. I like the contrast but am a city girl at heart – I need the cinema, theatre, restaurants, friends. It is very lovely here, though.

And I am reading fiction. Books by women with central female characters – really inspiring.

Tuesday 14 August

Lolita   It's Adrian's birthday. Goodness, how did we get here? Just a few minutes ago we were at RADA and now he's fifty. We have a lovely day. A real landmark of a birthday. Everything's the same but somehow, everything is also different.

Wednesday 15 August

Lolita   The joys of being on holiday, sitting around with nothing in your head but what to do and where to eat. These simple pleasures are not be underestimated. I can feel my batteries charging.

I am not allowing myself to dwell on the notes I got for *Pi*, or to wonder about what I may do for *Politically Correct*. I trust that my subconscious is working it out for me while I read and fill my head with other people's words.

Just finished Elena Ferrante's *The Lost Daughter*. It is brilliant. She expresses things you're not meant to say. It's the second of her books that I have read and I have gotten so wrapped up in her characters.

I have time for one more book before work demands my attention.

Was sent a potential audition for The Globe. It's an interesting project, short, over October and November, and perfectly doable with the writing I have on. It's a good part, which is great, but to learn that while I'm writing three scripts would be really hard. I said no. If I weren't writing, I would absolutely have gone for it. Choices have to be made.

Simon rang yesterday regarding *Pi*. Things are getting closer to a deal with Sheffield.

Saturday 18 August

Adrian   I'm on the plane as it returns to Gatwick.

I am officially middle-aged.

Fifty is a big solid number. Makes me think of silver-haired couples in adverts I saw when I was a kid. Once the nest is empty, their kids all grown up, they are smiling with sparkling dentures, free to travel wherever they like as they look over their pension plans and think about retirement.

The birthdays I've had with a zero in them have always forced me to do a bit of stocktaking. Have I achieved what I hoped I would? Am I the person I think I should be? It happened at thirty, just after Lolita and I got married, and it happened when I was forty, a dad with two children in school, and here I am doing it again at fifty while I'm sitting on a plane for a few hours as it heads for London.

My mind wanders, starts to draw a mental diagram of my life's plusses and minuses. It's like a chart tracking peace of mind as it tries to tell me whether it's ok to be this old when my age is measured up against the things I have and the things I will never get or have lost.

Like most people who are self-employed, nothing is constant. I have no idea where I will be six months from now. I don't know if I will be in the same country, what job I'll be doing, whom I'll be working for or with. I could be somewhere great working on good material or stuck somewhere doing something that's a big mistake. There's always a little insecurity that goes along with this adventure of possibility.

Another part of this self-employed environment is that your work prospects will always be rooted in some stranger's opinion of your abilities. For actors, the work isn't an external thing you can create and walk away from – it is you. You walk around wearing the face of your reputation. Good or bad. The more easily an actor is recognized by members of the public, the more power that actor has to command the interest of a potential audience when they are cast in something. The more of an audience you can command, the better your job prospects.

Sometimes actors can be chosen for a role simply because they have the right 'numbers'. More people know them in more international territories and these territories are important to the producers who need to sell the film, or TV show. Some producers will check to see how many social media followers an actor has. I thought that was ridiculous when I first heard it but now it makes sense. It tells the financial backers that you have a greater reach and that more people will watch the product. Many actors actively court social media followers so that they can have more cachet in getting roles on screen.

If performers are not that interested in getting as much social media attention as possible, they can feel that they are missing the boat. Attract followers, show your worth, get the part. Repeat.

No matter how proud I am of some of the things I've done there are times when the feeling that I am one of those that have missed the boat creeps up on me, stays for a while, and then disappears again. It happens. Happens to all my mates too.

But for me, the carrot that I might imagine always dangling in front of me isn't really about the jobs I could get, or the influential rooms and parties that I could get into. It's about the quality of the work I've done when a job is completed. I don't care where I'm employed. I always want the job that's going to make me a better actor. That's my carrot. A feeling that I have accepted a project or a role that gives me the chance to be better than I was before. I'm quite critical of myself. Out of all the jobs I've done, there are maybe one or two projects that

I'm completely happy with. The others, I believe, showed room for improvement.

With this attitude, I suppose it's understandable when people sometimes frown at me for not walking a path that could get me more attention.

The plane judders a little, bringing my thoughts back to where I'm sitting. I look around at my family spread out in different seats. Each of them reading, sleeping or listening to music. I stare at them. Rebalancing that fifty-year-old spreadsheet in my head.

No boats missed.

Monday 20 August

Lolita   I meet with Max and Simon at the Umbrella Rooms to do a few auditions for *Pi*. Initially it's for the workshop in September but with a longer view for the production as well.

Find out we are pretty much confirmed with Sheffield. Not everything is signed yet, but it's all falling into place. There's a scheduling issue about rehearsals. I am pushing for three weeks in London and two weeks in Sheffield because it would be easier for me with *Invisible Cities* rehearsing at the same time. I don't know if I'll get that, so will just have to work with what's given.

We talk through casting the next workshop in September and who to approach. Talk through logistics going forward. It's very exciting to be actually planning for a show that's going to happen.

It is the death of creativity not to work towards realization. So much work is done on spec, on the hope of it being produced. I remember after trying to move *Red Velvet*, the play, and all of those dead ends, when the door finally opened, I steamed through it.

It's been a long time since *Red Velvet*. It was first produced in 2012. It returned in 2014, then went to New York, off Broadway at St Ann's Warehouse. We returned in 2016 as part of Ken Branagh's season at the Garrick. It has had over twenty productions in America and I also did the radio version for BBC Radio 4, but I haven't had another play on and I am feeling it.

I am also aware that I don't want my acting to become secondary and that I need to keep that ball well up in the air.

Tuesday 21 August

Adrian   Went to the Raindance soirée where Terry Gilliam was to be given the auteur award.

As people mingled, eating canapés and waiting for things to get going, I met and had a nice chat with Peter Dunphy, the head of Gizmo Films, an independent film production company that is constantly on the lookout for films below a £2 million budget. I talk to him about a script that Lolita has been trying to get made for years. I am attached as director and we have had development money from the BFI. It's called *For Joy*. I talk him through the premise and the tone of the film. He finds the idea interesting and agrees to me sending it to him. He hands me a card. I don't believe he is simply being polite. Plus, I like the way he was talking about the other projects he is involved in.

After a few moments Elliot Grove, the head of Raindance, gets on the stage and kicks everything off with a great speech introducing Terry Gilliam.

Terry was, as usual, witty, irreverent and illuminating. He went through all of the departments that normally work on one of his films. He talked about the great ideas they've had and said that all he has to say is 'yes' and those ideas are now his!

'Isn't that a wonderful thing? If I say yes, then it's in my movie and if it's in my movie then woah . . . It had to be a Terry Gilliam idea!'

He then pointed out that if the idea is shit, he can say with a smile 'Great, we'll think about it,' and then elbow it later. He talked for about five minutes and then rounded everything up by saying to the giggling crowd, 'I'm not an *auteur*, I am a *filteur*. For everybody else's ideas. Ideas . . .' (he indicates Jonathan Pryce who is standing in the audience) '. . . that are better than mine and for which I get given the credit!'

Just listening to him makes me want to get behind the camera again.

On my way out of the Dorchester Hotel, I bump into Treva Etienne. Treva is an actor and director. It's been ages since I've seen him. To my mind, Treva is the original diversity and inclusion spokesman for film and TV in the UK. In 1996 he got fifty black actors and actresses – as well as Vanessa Redgrave – to have their picture taken standing behind a large banner that read 'OPPORTUNITY at the BAFTAs'. At that time, BAFTA really did look like an enclave of white film artists. Black attendance alone was remarkable, never mind black nominees. Treva was talking to funding bodies, government ministers and major TV companies. He warned of the lack of opportunity that artists face in their country of birth, and that it would lead to people leaving their home and going abroad to find work. I got the film *Primary Colors* the following year. Treva left Britain for America a few years after and has been living there ever since.

Diversity and inclusion seem to be buzzwords at the moment, with the 'Oscars So White' elements of the #MeToo campaign and diversity movements working daily to get things to change. I believe slow change is happening. But what concerns us all now is what happens when the complaints stop. Lasting change only comes when we change policy. Once that is done, people can stop campaigning and go back to making great work. Treva and others have spent over twenty years pushing for this stuff and only now is it beginning to really take hold.

Just like any other act of rebalancing, the industry has to push everything over to the opposite side for a while, to work on more inclusion, better and more diverse character breakdowns in scripts which casting directors then adhere to . . . all this needs to be done until the ship rights itself, and then hopefully, with new rules in place, we can carry on in a straight line. Actors should always (within reason) be able to play what they are not. But for far too many years, this rule only applied to white male actors.

I greet Treva – completely interrupting the conversation he is having. We spend a while catching up.

Treva has been working with Native American artists in Canada on drama. He wants to help a group get their stories told about how they are dealing with the fallout from, as he calls it 'the loss of a nation'. He still has that passion in his voice, that fire behind his eyes. He hasn't given up; he just moved. I leave him, making him promise to come round to the house and see Lolita and the kids before he heads back home to America.

Thursday 23 August

Lolita Was thinking about when my writing took off and people assumed I would give up my acting career to follow the words. I couldn't.

I love acting. I get frustrated by the lack of substantial roles – for my gender, my age, my race. But it is a frustratingly alluring profession.

It makes for a life of constant self-examination, where you constantly analyse your emotional responses, your abilities and place in the industry. You have to compete but stay balanced – too much negativity blocks your artistry. It is also a profession that can actively encourage the negative; it does not necessarily promote good self-esteem and stability. Against many odds, you need to stay as open as possible so that all emotional states are available to you so that when needed you can play anything.

When I produced *Of Mary* in 2010 with Rosa, which Adrian directed, I was on the other side of the camera and had to look after the actors. I realized then why actors are often treated with kid gloves. You need them to bring out raw feeling for the camera, so the environment around them needs to be as calm as possible.

I really like doing both disciplines. They feed into each other.

Saturday 25 August

Lolita   I just reread *Calmer*. I have a meeting about it next week and I haven't looked at it for a few months. I haven't written any of it for over a year.

It's always interesting going back to work after a gap because the absence of what you wanted to say becomes glaringly obvious. The central story is good and the relationships and characters are strong. It needs a more defined opening and a more satisfying finish though. Also one of the characters, Jude, who I think is essential but have struggled with, needs more. He needs a longer arc to get where he goes, as does the final denouement.

It's clear what I need to do next.

I gave this draft to the Old Vic and the Bridge Theatre. They came back with very positive feedback although it isn't a play for them, which I totally understand. One of them felt it was a studio piece. It's not what I intended so I will address that in the redraft.

Adrian   A day of photographs for *The Rook*'s marketing team. These things change so quickly.

We shot photos for posters in various contexts. Then I had to go to a different part of the studio for the 'gif' shoot – various movements lasting a few seconds that can be stitched together to contain more than one character or just be me on my own. Then we move on to the green screen set, where my image can be laid over any of the locations used in the shoot.

They even have ideas to make the adverts jump from one feed into another if you are on YouTube or using Twitter or Instagram. The company that came up with the idea have won an award for its eye-catching effectiveness. After all, the screen people stare at most is their phone.

All very exciting but, of course, this'll only matter if the series is good . . .

Monday 27 August

Lolita Am edging back into work.

I look through the notes on *Pi* I had from my meeting with Simon and Max. I am keen to have a restructured version for the workshop in two weeks. It's ambitious given that it is still the school holidays.

I am back in Nice for the last time next week and still haven't had a script. That will come when it comes.

Tonight I went to see *The King and I* at the London Palladium. My main reason was to see Ken Watanabe – a possibility for *Invisible Cities*.

The show was very well done but my God, it was so old fashioned. Like *42nd Street*, it gives the opportunity for a few big numbers – but the story creaks.

In the second half there was a play within the play, based on *Uncle Tom's Cabin*. It made me feel like I was either in a Monty Python sketch or a Terry Gilliam film.

I learned about Harriet Beecher Stowe's novel when I researched Ira Aldridge. It was a huge and unexpected hit – unusually for the time, written by a woman but also sympathetic to the slave characters it portrayed. Abolition was at its height so it played an important role in helping people see that 'slaves are people too'.

I haven't ever read this book but I know it was responsible for the phrase 'Uncle Tom', a stereotypical reference to a black person – lazy, smiling, fun, relaxed, happy with his lot. To say it is dated is a vast understatement.

In *The King and I*, the governess Anna tells the King that in order to show the emissary from England that he is 'civilized' and not a 'barbarian', they should wear Western dress and do this play.

So to see a twenty-minute showing of *Uncle Tom's Cabin* portrayed in what (we think) is a Siamese way of telling the story, where a runaway slave is chased by beautiful East Asian dogs, presented as a fun piece of theatre within theatre, was very strange. I was with my friend, who knew nothing of the history of Uncle Tom, and thought it was done beautifully. But this is the problem. If we iron over the truth of the past it becomes woven into a Eurocentric version of the future in which we become trapped. The truth is denied and the stereotypes prevail.

Having seen *The King and I* and *42nd Street* this summer, it makes me despair at the backward-looking, old-fashioned version of the world we are peddling. I haven't even mentioned how the women are presented in these pieces – one-dimensional, weak, obedient and 'good'.

Anyway, Ken Watanabe was great within the confines of the piece.

Tuesday 28 August

Lolita   I have a meeting with Chris Campbell, Literary Manager at the Royal Court, regarding *Calmer*.

Chris and I go way back. Twenty-odd years ago, we were in a disastrous production called *Dragon* at the National Theatre. We reminisce that it was possibly the worst job we had both ever done. People got fired or walked off it, there were arguments and factions and much drama off stage. It was good to see him and laugh.

He is very positive about my play and we talk about what it needs next. He says that the Court are not programming traditional plays like this at the moment. It's a four-act structure about a family. He therefore can't offer me anything more than the promise to read the next draft. I tell him of my frustrations, of having achieved so much with *Red Velvet* and then still having to jump through hoops. He is sympathetic. It is nice to be straight with him. Anyway – more hoops to jump through.

Wednesday 29 August

Lolita I meet with Max and a possible composer for *Pi* at a hotel near Oxford Circus. It is an interesting meeting and the guy's perspective on music within the show is strong.

Talking to Max afterwards, we try to define what kind of sound and feel we want for the show. I am very aware that it isn't my call, really. I also don't have that kind of eye for directing and never have. But I do have an instinct about which way to go. Felt careful of respecting Max's position whilst giving my opinion.

I find out that we won't get more than two weeks of rehearsal in London for *Pi*, so for three weeks of *Invisible Cities* I will have to travel up and down to Sheffield. It will be trickier but has to be done.

Sunday 2 September

Lolita At the end of play on Friday, I had two self-tapings emailed to me by my acting agents at Curtis Brown.

It's reassuring to have auditions, but with self-tapings I find myself squeezing them into times I should be doing something else.

It was a family affair today. I had three fairly hefty scenes for one audition and two short, sharp ones for a comedy pilot. They were very different styles.

Adrian is always brilliant and films, reads and directs me too. Jasmine joined us today and read as well.

There is so much prospecting in this industry – working hard in order to get the opportunity to audition for work. As I get older, I just want the work based on my track record.

Anyway, I did them. And then Adrian edited them and put them into files for my agent. I wouldn't know where to start if I had to do it by myself.

Thursday 6 September

Adrian Had a chat with Stephen Mears, the director on *Guys and Dolls* at the Royal Albert Hall.

I then went through the script. Should have done it much earlier. I have been neglecting this. Have to start the voice process and begin looking at the lines. At first, I thought we were going to do a rendition of the songs from the show: music stands in front of us, fixed microphones, little movement. Then I learned we would be doing some scenes as well. Ok, a little bit of dialogue to get us in and out of the songs – fine. But after talking to Stephen, I now understand why he wants us off book. The scenes will be fully acted and there's going to be a chorus of dancers as well. I'm flicking through the script, and there's a lot of lines. I have two solos, two duets, there are lots of scenes, costume, wigs, dance routines and only nine days' rehearsal.

This'll be . . . interesting.

Wednesday 5 September

Lolita   I am finishing a light structural redraft of *Pi* so that Simon and Max can read before Monday. Some of it works, some of it needs deeper thought. We are fully cast for the workshop, which is great. I have some more friends in this now too; they're good and nice people, so their support in the room is invaluable.

It is now the afternoon and I am having a long meeting with Leo, the director from 59 Productions, to get his thoughts on *Invisible Cities*. It is a good session, although getting my head back into the story takes a few moments. It's a fantastic piece for this kind of multi-performance expression but trying to find a narrative within it is hard. Anyway, Leo has some great ideas and problems so I will take them away and digest.

I am excited to hear The Armoury in New York is very interested in *Invisible Cities* for 2020 and Sadler's Wells want us to open their new space in London in Stratford in 2022. Also, apparently a lot of international venues are interested in the production and Rambert are keen to keep it in their repertoire, so it seems like it will have a long life.

I am working out dates for draft deliveries of *Invisible Cities* with Leo and we talk about sharing my time with rehearsals for *Pi*.

I have another audition tomorrow. A regular in a new series for ITV and the dates fit with what I'm doing. It's my third audition this week – am feeling very lucky to have so many opportunities. It stands in direct contrast to the many times I have had none.

I receive an email from Marcus Davey, artistic director at the Roundhouse, to talk about the idea I pitched to him. He wants to do it and to talk logistics. I want to do it with Alan Lane from Slung Low directing and Rosa Maggiora designing. So we're all going to meet in October and work it out. This will be fun.

Alan brought me back to the theatre, really. Almost ten years ago, I was pretty jaded by it. The experiences I'd had were hard and demoralizing. I was questioning my love of it. And then he asked me to write a monologue for his show at the Almeida. It was the first theatre piece I'd written that was produced and I also performed it. It was an event piece. Three writers, three monologues. The audience wore headphones and the actors wore microphones. We told a third of the audience our story and spent an hour walking the streets of Islington, where other actors and props were planted to support the narrative.

It was an extraordinary experience for me. The technology frequently went wrong but it was pure theatre. Pure storytelling. Alan has an infectious energy; he's a 'can do' person who makes anything happen, so to do this with him will be brilliant.

Rosa designed a show I was in around the same time at the Royal Court – *Free Outgoing* by Anupama Chandrasekhar. It was done on a minuscule budget. Rosa was instinctive and so responsive to what we needed. It was well received and came back to the main house and then went to the Traverse during the Edinburgh Festival. To work with her like this will be wonderful.

I am excited by this project – it is called *Testaments* – and it could be a bold and relevant piece of theatre, plus I'll be working with good friends.

Friday 7 September

Lolita   I am filming my last scene on *Riviera*. This has been a fun job to do – great costumes and sets. The part has been frustrating as it demands very little but I have enjoyed it.

Monday 10 September

Lolita   This is the first day of the second workshop on *Pi*. We have ten actors, Max, Finn (puppet and movement director) and Yann Martel – author of the book. We are in a rehearsal room in Bethnal Green working through my last draft to try and find the story arc of the whole piece. Each scene must inform the next, build to a climax and deliver an emotional journey at the same time. It's linking many threads until they become one rope – sort of.

I am nervous because I am being put through my creative paces but being surrounded by so many creative minds will feed my vision. It is a great day of seeing where the gaps are and being presented with ideas of how to fill them.

Yann has come over from Canada to be here for the week. I am amazed at how generous he is being with this opus of his. He is very open to my reinvention of his story.

I am more sure-footed this time, I think. Ready for the chaos of this week. It feels like throwing the whole script, story and order up in the air and seeing where it lands.

Thursday 13 September

Adrian   On my way in to do a demo for a large commercial radio station today. It's a try-out, a mutual audition to see if my voice and manner would work well for their audience and to see if I can handle the technical aspects needed for the work.

Ever since I started doing voice-overs for TV documentaries, I have been loosely interested in the idea of doing radio. A few actors have done the job as they are able to bring an entertaining slant on current affairs all while presenting listeners with a good selection of music.

In preparation I'd had a lot of ideas about the little stories I might tell the audience, the news references I could talk about or make light of and especially the music that I would like to play.

Seems slightly obvious to say that the music was a big draw. Years ago I had listened to Lenny Henry on the radio make his turn as a DJ a unique listening experience. He recorded himself as a character who had phoned in or entered the booth interrupting and chatting away to himself as Lenny the DJ. It was a free-wheeling conversation that was very surreal and very funny. The tracks he played, chatted over and sometimes sang along to all helped to make his show unique. I felt that, given the opportunity, I would be able to create a show that had a similar sense of fun with good conversation, and above all good music. I'm not sure about doing it, so having the chance to test things out seems like a very good idea.

I arrive with Tina, our personal manager. I'm greeted by the producer of my hour and then settled down at a desk with a mic. As I start to talk about the songs I think would be good and the various intros I could build around each one (I had made a list), the producer asks me if I got the list of songs they sent over. I admit that I had but thought it was sent as a note for the kind of tone that could be used. He now hands me the list again and this time with a script for the various intros to each track.

I had prepared my own intros and talking points. But I had to accept that radio DJs don't pick the music they play on a commercial station and each link between the tracks is timed to be anything between five or thirty seconds. Any kind of take I had on the music wasn't up for discussion. The music that will be played at a particular moment in the show is issued two days before, along with the suggested time in the day for the track to be played. I couldn't influence anything, I would just be able to make the polite chit-chat in between, and even that had some hefty parameters to it. I feel disappointed and a little stupid for not realizing this earlier. I knew the station and its taste in mood and music but hadn't realized how the whole thing might be put together.

I love music. It's always been a big part of my life. I can find a song to listen to at any point in the day to fit any mood. I even have music I listen to when I don't want to listen to music.

It started with me getting into dance when I was six or seven years old, then joining a cathedral choir at nine. For a good few years I would go to church on a Sunday morning to sing during a Latin mass – Mozart, Haydn, Purcell, Bach – then get home, change into tracksuit and trainers and get myself over to the Midlands Arts Centre to practise windmills and backspins to Mann Parrish, Afrika Bambaataa, Newcleus and Herbie Hancock.

As I'm on my way home from the radio station, I feel it's been a wasted journey. This is all far too scripted and fixed. I also thought I would be in control of playing the songs, bringing them in and fading them down for a comment or a joke. Seems like I'd spent too long listening to pirate radio stations. A DJ at a party has more control than this.

Friday 14 September

Lolita   It is the last day of the workshop. It has been intense but helpful. Between us we acted out the whole script as it stands and worked out the dramatic beats in each scene that will spur the story on. Max is very clear about what needs to be underneath each scene in order to progress the whole story through. The actors have been great – really engaged in working out the knots in the story and discussing the overall themes and possibilities for each scene. They've also been very game in getting up and doing it.

So I am left with a million notes, a progressive scene structure through the play and a strong set of visual images to place the story on. Finn's work with the prototype puppets and the work he's done on the visual language is absolutely magical. It transforms the story. All these creative minds working to tell a story is a humbling thing.

So I must make the script better in order to give everyone a good springboard from which to work. This has been a tough, rigorous week but it is very exciting.

I am offered a small part in a low-budget film Ken Branagh is directing in October. It's called *All Is True*. The part is very modest, but it is always lovely just to be offered something and I know it will be fun to do.

Tuesday 18 September

Adrian   Cycled across town to meet Andrina Linnell at Body & Soul, a charity based on Rosebery Avenue that supports children and their families whose lives have been affected by HIV and AIDS. Lolita and I are long-time supporters of the work they do.

We have, in the past, heard stories of the children who are under three years old and too young to realize what being HIV-positive means. Back then there were the kids at primary school, fully aware of their condition, who had to be careful around other children while taking a cocktail of ten or more pills at timed intervals throughout the day – that was how they used to manage the condition.

Now, Andrina tells me, most of those who access their services with the disease are taking only one or two pills a day.

Body & Soul has recently widened its remit. It now helps people who are dealing with the life-threatening effects of childhood adversity – children coping with drug abuse, for either themselves or a parent, depression, suicidal thoughts and other mental issues. Whether people have been neglected, abused, trafficked, stigmatized or have attempted suicide because of HIV, Body Soul is there for them. So much so that the charity now has over 5,000 people who access their services.

As Andrina shows me around the relatively small building they have, I read poetry written by some of the kids, look at drawings and listen to Andrina tell me about some of the cases that come through the door.

The late Anita Roddick was a fervent supporter of the charity. I saw a quote of hers on a wall as we walked around (I believe it was originally said by Desmond Tutu): 'Giving to charity is the rent I pay for living on the planet.' I leave the building moved by the scope of their work and let them know again that as well as donations, if they need me to make speeches or lobby people on their behalf, they should just let me know.

Lolita I am in Belfast recording a radio play called *Swans* by Eoin McNamee, for BBC Radio 4. It is directed by my mate Celia. I arrived yesterday and recorded some scenes. It's about child-trafficking in Dublin. It's an interesting group of actors, a very different community of people; all of them are Irish and immersed in the industry on this side of the water. I realize how London-centric things get. Not healthy at all.

I wake early today at 6.00 am and start to put my *Pi* workshop notes in order. There are loads of them and they're very detailed. I have breakfast at the hotel and do a little more work but only get halfway through my notes by the time I have to pack up, check out and get to the studio to start recording.

I record all day. Then I go to the airport where I finish off the other half of my *Pi* notes. On the plane I look at this diary to see if I am making sense.

Wednesday 19 September

Lolita   I spend the morning looking at *Pi*. I have collated all the notes from the workshop and written out the new structure, now I move all the pieces of the puzzle to make sure it has a strong emotional drive to the narrative. It requires focus and time but the work from the workshop is strong in my head. As I am writing the first scene in the hospital, the elements of the story feel clear and the relationships between the characters are becoming more specific and defined. I like this stage – the excavation becomes more detailed and the revelations subtler.

It's the afternoon and I am driving to Longcross Studios in west London to have a make-up/hair test and meet Ken Branagh for the small part I am doing in his film *All Is True*. I am playing a landlady of a tavern in Stratford. I have two modest scenes. I really enjoy working with Ken because he demands the best of you and is intrinsically creative. The detailed questions he asks of me for these two small scenes make me feel like I have something to contribute.

My hair test is good and gives me a flavour of the film. It's about Shakespeare so is set in seventeenth-century England. Great to see the make-up designer's pictures of reference included black and Asian women of that time. That's a first. I come away really looking forward to my couple of days on this in October.

Friday 21 September

Adrian   Final day of shooting on *The Rook* at 3 Mills Studios in north-east London. The director China Moo-Young made it a swift morning – one scene completed in two great set-ups with a few changes of camera lens. She had obviously really thought it all out and planned her shots. I am always watching the directors I work with always trying to learn from the good and the bad.

I say my goodbyes and jump into a car to get me over to the *Guys and Dolls* photo shoot, which is happening not too far away.

As I walk in, the shoot is already underway. Joe Stilgoe, Cory English, Jason Manford and Clive Rowe (who I have not been on stage with since the Sondheim musical *Company* at the Donmar Warehouse twenty-one years ago), are getting dressed up into 1930s suits and fooling around in front of the camera with our director Stephen Mear.

A couple of the guys had done it before and are happy to do a concert version. Jason and I haven't, though, and are a little more apprehensive about how to get the songs and dialogue in our heads so fast. We basically have ten days before the orchestra joins us and we are then put on to that massive stage at the Royal Albert Hall.

Clive tells us all about LineLearner, an app that helps you learn lines in various combinations and speeds. I ask him if there is a way I can get the music for my solos, so that I can practise them without someone else singing. I need to get a little used to singing the songs without the lead line being fed to me by an instrument or another person's voice. Clive quickly responded, 'oh yeah, just go onto YouTube and put in the name of the show and song in karaoke and a few versions will come up'.

I thanked him. It was such a simple answer. I had heard tracks played out like that online before, why hadn't I thought of it? It's probably because the last time I did a musical on stage and needed that kind of research, the internet wasn't sophisticated enough to deliver it. The technology wasn't available for people to post that kind of thing. Soon, those of us who can remember the world without mobile phones or the internet will be the true marker for old age. People will go onto chat shows and describe a world before search engines and social media and the audience will gasp and applaud.

Sunday 23 September

Adrian   Lolita and I are at the Stage Debut Awards, an awards ceremony where *The Stage* newspaper recognizes great performances from actors who have just entered the profession. It's a chance to reward young practitioners, so many of whom were genuinely bowled over by an acknowledgement from the wider industry of their hard work so far. It felt good to be part of a ceremony that lets young artists know that their work in Salisbury, Cheltenham or Suffolk can get them recognized at a ceremony by a national publication. It removes the disconnect between those who always feel they have to work in the capital to push their careers forward. Cush Jumbo was a very funny and sincere host.

Tuesday 25 September

Adrian   I am at the Roundhouse Chairman's dinner with Lolita this evening in aid of raising funds and profile for the great work the Roundhouse does with young people. This place always reminds me of the Midlands Arts Centre in Birmingham, where I discovered my love for acting. A place that was cheap enough for young people to come to every day, to use the facilities and practise their chosen performance discipline.

I'm sitting next to Justine Simons, the Deputy [London] Mayor for Culture and the Creative Industries, who works very closely with Sadiq Khan. We start talking about all of the negative xenophobic rhetoric that was bandied about during the 2016 referendum and what the cultural landscape of London might look like after Brexit. We agree that it would be good to try and reset the capital's image of itself, to focus less on what divides us and more on what joins us.

I'm a romantic when it comes to views of society and cohesion. I was glad to get the opportunity to talk to her.

Lolita   At the Roundhouse Chairman's dinner, Adrian and I are sat on artistic director Marcus' table – it is always nice to see him.

Some of the emerging performers from the Roundhouse do a show – its choir, a musician, poets, presenters. It is good to be reminded of what the Roundhouse stands for and of the size and scale of their space. It gives me ideas for *Testaments*, the project I am developing for them.

Wednesday 26 September

Adrian   I have my first music rehearsal with James McKeon, our musical director on *Guys and Dolls*. A film crew are going to turn up and shoot some of it for use on *The One Show* and social media.

I feel I have a good grasp of the songs and the material, but nevertheless I always feel that little pull of nerves when I have to get up and prove it. Especially given that putting a first rehearsal on camera feels doubly exposing.

Anyway, it'll be a good chance to record a few more vocal warm-ups and workouts. I've been using the same ones for years.

It's a few hours later now and the rehearsal seemed to go well. There's a difference between singing a version of a popular musical song the way everyone thinks it goes and sitting down at a piano to have a 'note bash' – meticulously working out the correct time signatures and pitch. It always surprises me that in order to learn a song from a musical, you first have to *unlearn* the version of somebody else singing it that you have in your head. The camera crew were unobtrusive and allowed James and I to keep working.

I'm walking away from the session now with all of my songs recorded. I will listen to them over and over before we start on the 8th. I've been in touch with a few of the cast over social media where we have all shared our nerves at attempting to do this with such little rehearsal. I suppose it's good to be tested like this; sharpens everything up.

Lolita   I meet up with actress friend Kim Vithana, who is taking me and another friend to London Zoo. She has a friend there who is an animal behavioural specialist and thought he might be useful for my *Pi* research. She is right. It is a beautiful sunny day and the zoo is an amazing place. We see a tiger, meerkats, zebras and giraffes, and I speak to an orangutan keeper too. It is really useful to see the animals and to hear about their tendencies. Made me see that the scenes in *Pi* where the animals are stuck on the boat will need to have a stronger sense of danger.

We spend the whole day at the zoo seeing other animals, too. The size and power of the zebra is very striking, but the keeper describes them as prey and not predators. It gives an immediate sense of a zebra's priorities. The keeper said that if a zebra were hurt, as in *Pi*, it would stay silent so as not to attract predators.

It is a day well spent.

Monday 1 October

Lolita   I have done all the workshop notes for *Pi*, restructured the whole piece and been specific about the cost and pay off of each event that happens. The book is packed with wonderful scenarios and visual story, but the building of intent is not there.

Today I am reading back on what I've done. It's very different and tighter in places – particularly the Okamoto and Lulu Chen story. The scenes jump, though, and I'm not sure whether that works yet. Have to keep the faith and plough on.

I love the playful and mischievous way religion is discussed in the book. It is done with total respect and humour. The problem with transposing that into drama is that it has no drive. So whilst religion is crucial to the story-telling, how do you talk about god and devotion without it sounding either tub-thumping or dull? Anyway, I think I'm getting closer. It is part of a scene about the family, rather than a long-considered examination of Christianity, Islam and Hinduism.

I am enjoying solving the problems, but my head aches at the end of the day.

Tuesday 2 October

Adrian   Luke Redgrave and I have a meeting with Callum Grant of AGC Studios and his assistant, Samuel Hall. They have read the latest version of *Lottery Boy* and wanted to have a meeting to discuss. Luke and I aren't sure what the agenda is here, but understand that if AGC Studios like the project we could, after a few crucial meetings, receive the entire budget packaged by them and be in pre-production in a few months. Callum and Samuel are very straightforward, down-to-earth guys who are talkative and happy to meet.

We speak about *Lottery Boy* in great detail. Callum is very clear in his appreciation of the script and what elements he thinks work. I begin telling him what I'm planning to do with the next draft, hoping that he likes it enough to officially jump on board in some way. Even though this is an informal chat, I know I'm pitching my film to him. I can feel myself listen to every word I say and judge each word I choose. I'm wary of him looking at me or away from me or becoming disinterested or any other sign that might tell me during my 'pitch' how interested he finally might be. I finish by summing up exactly what I think the finished product will look like in the marketplace, who would watch it, what value it has at the cinema etc. Callum remains very positive but noncommittal. Looks like he's going to wait and see what happens with this next draft and whether I can deliver what I say I can.

We then begin talking about *Hustle*, which he says was one of his all-time favourite shows. He asks if there is a possibility for a film? I explain that Tony Jordan, the show's creator, had been around the houses with a film version but no one had fully bitten. I think that since the *American Hustle* film and various heist movies have all hit the screens, maybe the idea had been overtaken by time, but end by telling him that *Hustle* was unique with it's ingenious plotting and could really do with a big screen moment. He tells me that if I wanted to direct a movie of *Hustle* he would be 100 per cent behind it.

Just as I start to feel that perhaps *Lottery Boy* isn't the real purpose of this meeting. Callum begins to chat about *Lottery Boy*, noting its unique take on the rags-to-riches genre. He tells me that anybody who wants to sell the film will be pushing it to have the same elements as other successful movies in that vein but that my script's selling point is its emotional centre. He says that other movies do stunts or stars and all the other stuff that gets material sold, but that this film will break your heart. He thinks that as long as we stay true to that in the next draft, we'll be off and running. I feel greatly encouraged and as they leave to get back to the office, Luke and I sit and talk through what the next draft could be and what we should do with it.

In the evening I go along to the Universal screening rooms off Shaftesbury Avenue to see *Mary Queen of Scots* for the first time and thoroughly enjoy it. I play Lord Thomas Randolph, Queen Elizabeth I's ambassador to Scotland. It was one of those dream jobs that falls into your lap, in this case a call from Josie Rourke out of the blue asking if I would take part. We shot it last summer. It was interesting to see myself playing an Elizabethan alongside all the other actors. It is the first time in my thirty-year career I have been cast in a period drama. My race is not relevant to the story. I enjoy the film. It is a very good retelling of history from a different perspective. Saoirse Ronan, Margot Robbie, Jack Lowden and the cast all give fine performances. It's a great debut film from Josie Rourke. Fingers crossed for how well it does on release.

Wednesday 3 October

Lolita   I am at Sydenham High School for Girls this morning. It's Black History Month and I talk about Ira Aldridge to the whole school at assembly. It goes well, I think, though sometimes I have so much to say I think I jump between subjects without properly explaining the context. Anyway – dear Ira. It was lovely to talk about him with young minds. That's how he travels on.

I spend the afternoon writing *Pi*. I have put in all the workshop notes but they lack emotional logic so now I need to go back over them again. It's hard, trying to give every line an intention and emotional journey. It's coming, though. I was a bit cross-eyed with staring at the computer by the time I'd finished.

And then in the evening Adrian and I see *Tina – The Tina Turner Musical*. It is a great night out. A completely different demographic of audience to what I am used to fills the theatre. The lead actress was amazing – she took the roof off the Aldywch. It was brilliant to see the talent of the rest of the cast too. The company was composed of a lot of black actors, mostly women: it's a rare sight and every single one of them was strong. Feel very uplifted by it.

Adrian At a performance of *Tina – The Tina Turner Musical*, directed by Phyllida Lloyd. Lolita and I are both completely in awe of Adrienne Warren's voice. Man, that woman can sing! I've been starting each day with a stretch and a vocal workout for my voice as I get ready for *Guys and Dolls*. I sit watching Adrienne thinking 'How the hell is she doing that?'

Afterwards, we had a little laugh to ourselves when we realized that both of the major theatres on that block in the West End were playing Phyllida's shows: *Mamma Mia* was next door. Phyllida had worked with both Lolita and myself at the Royal Exchange Theatre in Manchester when she was associate director there about twenty-five years ago. Now she has a block in the West End.

Thursday 4 October

Adrian Watched *Othello* at Shakespeare's Globe Theatre and afterwards I meet with André Holland, who played the title role. We talk in great detail about the character and how certain elements are extremely uncomfortable to play. The ferocity of the jealousy defies logic and therefore makes it very difficult to get lost in Othello's story night after night. André talks a little about being directed by Claire van Kampen, Mark Rylance's wife, and how, because of their deep understanding of each other's approach to the work, André felt like Iago's story framed the play. Iago is the only character that speaks directly to the audience and so his jaded point of view is the basis for our acceptance and understanding of the other characters. It is very hard for the actor playing Othello to rebalance that with credibility and as we talk I see once again how unsettling this role can be.

The Globe's Head of Education, Farah Karim-Cooper, joins us afterwards. We always get on well and are soon chatting extremely loudly in the bar. I remember being very, very tempted by the formal interest for me to put myself forward for the job of artistic director at The Globe. The approach has put an idea in my mind that has taken hold and now won't go away. Not now and not for The Globe, where Michelle Terry is currently doing a fantastic job of reimagining the theatre's approach to the classics, but I keep turning the idea over in my head. What theatre could I run? What would I do? How would I reinvigorate what goes on there . . .?

I enjoyed the very present and involved feel of the crowd while watching André and Mark Rylance on stage, and I imagine how the version of *Cyrano* I am working on would play in this theatre. The interplay with the audience, the sword-fighting, the huge romance and declarations of honour and pride. I think it would work well. I mention it to Farah, asking her to keep it quiet. She loves the idea and puts me in touch with Michelle Terry.

I float the idea past producer James Bierman and director Simon Evans, who both think it would work well in the space and so I send Michelle the script. She promises to read it ASAP even though she is in rehearsals for *Macbeth* at the moment.

Friday 5 October

Adrian Media day with Tina doing various bits of PR for *Guys and Dolls*. I have an interview with Clive Anderson for *Loose Ends* on BBC Radio 4. Jeff Goldblum is another guest and plays live with the Mildred Snitzer Orchestra. I had no idea how good a pianist he is. Jeff sits down to jam and plays piano much like he acts, as if each new chord change or every note picked in a solo is a complete surprise to him. Always fresh and entertaining.

Afterwards, Graham Norton chatted about his new novel and how he felt people might have to adjust to him writing a very serious story. Jeff Goldblum plays jazz piano and Graham Norton writes novels. Who knew? Lots of people, apparently. We finish the programme with Jeff and the band doing another set before I have to go over to do a pre-record of an interview with Steve Wright for his radio show.

Lolita   Just finished my draft of *Pi*!!!! Whooop! I have a small plateau of calm now until Monday, when I start the next draft of *Invisible Cities*. I have an audition this afternoon for a TV drama and haven't been able to focus on it – too many lines of story in my head.

Monday 8 October

Adrian   First day of rehearsals for *Guys and Dolls*. I cycle over to the rehearsal rooms in Pimlico. Finally get to meet the full cast this morning, including Lara Pulver, who is playing Sarah Brown – all of my songs, except 'Luck Be A Lady', are with her. Stephen Mear gets us off to a great start by explaining what will be happening in the show, where the orchestra will be, how we come off and on, what he expects us to aim for in the final show, but all with the caveat that we must in the end be comfortable and be relaxed about it all. He is straightforward, practical and obviously has a million things in his head but is calm and funny. He answers a few questions then gets us all together for a read-through. Lara is lovely, has a beautiful voice, is very easy going and really open to new ideas. Jason Manford as Nathan Detroit is the same. In fact, the entire cast are great to work with.

Tuesday 9 October

Adrian   Second day of rehearsals. Clive Rowe is, of course, brilliant as Nicely-Nicely Johnson. His 'Sit Down, You're Rockin' the Boat' is beginning to be the stuff of theatrical legend and I can't wait to see what he and the dancers have cooked up. Jason Manford and I have a little moan that we don't have any songs together. There are some great voices in the room and I'm in awe at how fast the dancers learn choreography and work off of each other at a moment's notice.

At lunchtime I run off to have a meeting with Eric Collins, who wants to spearhead a new venture capital company that will launch a fund to help BAME-led companies in media, health, lifestyle and the digital industries. It will provide access to the money they need to get their ideas off the ground. He tells me that Lenny Henry and others attended a meeting with businessman Tom Ilube during which the conversation turned to trying to find a solution for the fact that black business enterprises are statistically less likely to attract the money they need to launch or develop their business ideas. In this way, start-ups and other new companies led by BAME people in Europe don't have the support that their counterparts have. There is an obvious gap and Eric thinks we can fill it if we only have the guts to jump in. Eric is brilliant at explaining it all. He wants investment from me. Of course.

I have to be very careful here. It's venture capital and is therefore very risky.

Lolita I am writing *Invisible Cities* this morning, incorporating Leo's notes. It's a very different process to *Pi*. Leo's notes are more spatial, pictorial, about shapes of character that denote their journeys. It's nice to come back to it, though. As I refer to the novel, I see how much I have had to invent story and drive but retain the essence of the novelist, Calvino. I am taking his words and literally weaving them into my narrative.

In the afternoon, I meet with two women who have asked me to be a trustee for the Royal Victoria Hall Foundation. They award grants to London theatre companies and drama students. In fact, one of their earliest awards went to Adrian while he was still at RADA over thirty years ago, and he says it made a real difference to him. I hear a bit about their work and then agree to become a trustee.

Then I go to see an art exhibition of friends of mine. The artist, Shivinder, used to be an actor but some years ago suffered a life-threatening heart attack that meant he was unable to keep acting. He has reinvented himself through his art, which he is now pursuing with the dedicated support of his actress wife, Alison, who I worked with many years ago. I go to see his exhibition in central London. It is beautiful work, completely reflecting his experience. It is part graphic novel, part technical fantasy and part spiritual awakening. It is good to catch up with them too.

Afterwards I meet Monica Dolan, an actress friend, and we go to the press night of *Height of the Storm* at Wyndham's Theatre, which Simon (*Life of Pi*) is producing. Consummate performances. Effortless acting. Made me realize that a lifetime of working at your craft gets you to a place where you make it look easy. Just that. Nothing more.

Friday 12 October

Lolita   This morning I am doing some more detailed work on *Invisible Cities*. Because it's a relatively short piece made up of vignettes, it's quite intense. So I push on through it all before taking a break.

Then in the afternoon I begin the first draft of *Politically Correct*, my adaptation of a French play. I've been thinking about it for a while but not had the time to properly set any of my thoughts down.

The story itself is quite simple but the setting is complex. It's about two single people meeting and starting a relationship, while an election takes place in which the right wing slowly gain a lot of ground. It has the space to have much discussion about political loyalty and choices. It's particularly relevant at this time.

It is equal parts scary and exhilarating to start my version of a new piece. The basic story of the French play is sound but it needs a lot of character reinvention within it. You do all this prep and lots of study and then at some point you just have to take a leap and start.

Saturday 13 October

Adrian   A few weeks ago I got invited to become a member of the Academy of Motion Picture Arts and Sciences (AMPAS). I was honoured and accepted straight away. Now Lolita and I are at the Oscars new members' reception in London. A cool event with some very nice speeches being made.

A photo was taken of us all and it was a nice feeling that so many women and people of colour were being included. Obviously AMPAS was aware that its membership globally had to change, it's just a shame this realization came after strong criticism. I truly believe that if things had gone on as they had before with the lack of diversity in film and the disparity between what male and female stars are paid, AMPAS members and the Oscars ceremony itself, as a celebration of all of these things, risked becoming irrelevant.

Monday 15 October

Lolita I go for a run. I started running again last week and find it essential for these intense periods of writing. Sitting at the computer all the time with your own thoughts becomes very solitary. I don't like running, but I need it to balance the way I'm working at the moment.

I write *Invisible Cities* again this morning. I've restructured it and am finding a way of writing it specifically for all the disciplines involved – which parts should be spoken, which parts should be movement and which parts should be digital. Now I am putting in character, intent, story and setting it in some really spectacular places. I let my imagination fly completely, knowing Leo will restrict it afterwards.

I go into 59 Productions for a casting meeting. Sam Jones is casting. I've known her a long time. She cast me as an actress in *Beowulf* for ITV and *To Provide All People* for the BBC. She's very good in the auditions – always feels like she is on the actor's side. It is great to sit with her, Leo and Mai, who is producing for MIF, and talk through ideas and possibilities. I love casting. Actors always bring a different perspective to what you've imagined and the right actors make it live.

Thursday 18 October

Adrian More *Guys and Dolls* rehearsals, more standing in the corner in wonder at the skill of the dancers and singers in the room. Clive Rowe sang 'Sit Down, You're Rockin' The Boat' today. They have been working on it for a few days with no one else in the room. Now other members of the cast sit around the edges watching, eager to see what they have been up to. The dancers are filling in the gospel-led vocals while spinning, jumping and jiving around him. I can feel the hairs stand up on the back of my neck as Clive leans back into the high notes, smiling at us all as, with a gesture or a beat in the bar, a skilled dancer launches into a spin or a jump as if, almost, at his command.

We stand and applaud afterwards. Flippin' ace.

The 'sitzprobe' follows in the afternoon – the first time we get to sing with the orchestra. It marks a huge change from rehearsing with just a piano. Suddenly there is a wall of sound that carries the song with you. Today it is so easy to see why and how musicals work. The orchestra are fantastic. No matter what happens with my work in the future, I know I will never stop doing this.

Lolita I am finding it hard going writing *Invisible Cities* and *Politically Correct* at the same time. The first project is, in reality, just a conversation between two men where nothing really happens. While it's important to retain the languid quality of Calvino's work, it is in direct opposition to what is needed for the stage adaptation. And with the second project I am going through the often unfulfilling loose and rough marking-out of territory stage, which is always hard to do.

So I am delighted that today I get to do my other job. I am driven out to Windsor for a costume fitting for *All Is True* before I film next week.

I return home to wade through some more of the two plays and also have a conversation with an Italian translator for *Invisible Cities*. Leo wants Marco Polo to speak another language and Italian seemed the obvious choice. The translator seems very nice and capable.

I sometimes worry when I have to work as an actor while writing a project that I will waste time and be too split in focus to fulfil my writing deadlines. But it is great to be reminded how these two disciplines feed each other. I love acting. It's about a freedom to play, whilst writing is freedom of thought. So to step away from my desk where I scrutinize every word and instead do the 'proper' job that I trained for is a welcome relief and releases the cobwebs that gather because of my newer profession of choice.

Friday 19 October

Adrian *Guys and Dolls* opened at the Royal Albert Hall this evening. The place was full. Singing on that stage with the Royal Philharmonic Orchestra behind us was breathtaking.

I think nearly my entire family was there. The stage and venue is so big that I could hear a slight delay to the sound made by my voice coming back at me from the auditorium. In fact, there's an extra delay to everything when listening to the crowd – to their laughter, their applause – and the music. It's important to be able to listen well because you have to know when to allow for a laugh so that you can continue speaking as it hits a crest and begins to die down. It affects comic timing.

All of this is just me getting used to playing such a large venue with so little rehearsal. We were allowed into the theatre for the first time this morning and now we are running around for our exits and entrances backstage in time to the music with a full audience.

It's a great experience and it means a lot to me that Lolita, Lila, Jasmine and more family members are able to come along and see it.

Lolita   Jasmine and I arrive at the Royal Albert Hall to see *Guys and Dolls*. Lila is seeing it tomorrow with a friend. We find the rest of the family and have a quick catch-up.

The show is absolutely spectacular. The sound of the orchestra is so full it feels like we are immersed in one of those romantic movies from the 1940s. The actors have the audience in the palm of their hands. You can see that they are having a good time on stage, which helps us sit back and really enjoy the show. The dancers are wonderful. The fact that there are only three performances makes it a very special night out.

Adrian sings and dances with great charm. I can tell he is having fun. He is always very different with every character he plays and so detailed. Jasmine and I were very proud indeed.

Tuesday 23 October

Lolita   Picked up at 5.30 am and driven to Windsor to film *All Is True* today. I know a lot of the cast. Ken often hires actors he's worked with before, people with whom he has already established a sense of trust. There's a lovely feeling on set. Some of the actors from *Hamlet* in which I played Gertrude and Ken was director are in it and a couple of those actors are here today. It is so nice to get away from my desk and do this. I am wigged up, strapped into my seventeenth-century clothes and brought over to the beautiful sixteenth-century house we are filming in.

Ken's make-up to play William Shakespeare is quite extraordinary and he looks unrecognisable. There are a strange few moments on set where you glance over and see Shakespeare dressed in his doublet and hose directing us all from behind the camera.

Ken's attention to the detail of acting, his knowledge of shots and what he wants to see while he's playing a major role is admirable.

Thursday 25 October

Lolita   I finish my new draft of *Invisible Cities*.

I have found it difficult. I put in the notes that Leo gave me about shifts of power and physical shapes of character in relation to each other. I made the stakes of the scenes clearer and tried to make sure each character, while finding their journey through the piece, also fought for supreme status.

After a while I am unable to see the wood for the trees. I take a step back and realize that I am trying to stay true to Calvino's book. But his book is about a long, philosophical conversation between two men that incorporates many strange and wonderful cities but there is nothing at stake. There is very little progression dramatically.

So in putting a story and drive within it, I have to tread carefully to retain Calvino's intentions. Drive and malaise are in opposition. Trying to be progressive with static description is tricky but I think I've done the best I can for now in marrying these two elements.

I have also broken up the script into dance, movement, digital projection as well as dialogue. I am aware that artists of different disciplines will be reading my script to find their story. The responsibility of doing all this while holding on to a narrative is sobering.

Anyway, I have sent it off. Now I have to wait for everyone's thoughts.

Wednesday 31 October

Adrian   Spending most of today going through *We Prey*, an unproduced script for a three-part TV series that Lolita and I wrote in 1999, to see if the plot would work well for a possible shift into the pilot for a new drama series that I'm thinking about. I spend a few hours on it and then send it off to Karen Wilson at Kudos, executive producer of *Hustle*. I write a long email with the document attached, spelling out the plot and tone of the three episodes written but also incorporating the possible ways in which we could keep the story turning for future episodes.

Once that has been sent, I take a short break from the screen before working on another pilot idea.

I am also bouncing emails back and forth with Marcus Ryder, Lenny Henry, Pat Young and Meera Syal. We are going to take a letter to Downing Street calling for a Representation Tax Relief for the film and TV industry. Ofcom have just presented their 2018 figures on how well the broadcasters are doing with their work in front of and behind the camera. Things are moving far too slowly. Representation in front of the camera is getting much better, but without change *behind* the camera it is not enough. We have to keep up pressure on Ofcom and the major broadcasters.

Thursday 1 November

Adrian Frank Langella is in town and we meet to catch up over brunch. We worked together eleven years ago in New York on an independent film called *Starting Out in the Evening* that was written and directed by Andrew Wagner and have kept in touch ever since. Frank is eighty now. So much experience wrapped up in his jokes and observations. We talk about family, friends and work. He is still asking questions, still curious and searching.

We talk about my desire to play *Cyrano*, the context, the other characters. Frank has played Cyrano three times and has used different translations. He is convinced that audiences are ignorant when it comes to colour and that their first touch point when looking at the Cyrano, Christian and Roxanne love triangle will be obvious assumptions based on colour or age. He wonders why I don't make it an all-black cast. Then he says: 'They will see him as a man, not a black man onto which they will add lots of ignorant judgments.'

We talk further and I explain my reasons behind certain choices I have already made with the casting. But, however much I talk, I am explaining, explaining why it's ok for me to play this role while accepting the judgements that will be placed on me. Frank is aware of this too and begins to call potential audiences insulting names when he refers to them in our conversation.

The play shows us a man who is not judged based on the beautiful content of his mind but on the way everyone reacts to his appearance. If we want to make a comment on society by underlining that negative judgement with skin colour, then ok, fine. Not earth-shattering, but it has legs. The problem starts when Roxanne, the object of Cyrano's love, does not desire him but desperately wants Christian. If she is white, in my mind, the comment being made about race is quite strong. In this context, what should Christian be?

'All we have to do,' I say with a grin, 'is make sure we find an audience and critics for every performance who would never judge colour as character'.

'Hello . . .? Earth calling Adrian. Earth calling . . .'

We smile and tuck into our food.

Conversations about diversity and race have followed me at every step throughout my career.

Every part I have ever played has been accompanied by questions of colour. Whether I've done a musical on stage, a TV drama or a film, I have always had to answer questions from journalists asking me to talk about how they see the colour of my skin and what it means to them. Sometimes, of course, the colour and culture of the person I'm playing is relevant to the story but at other times it really isn't.

Some comments attempt to come as a form of praise, telling me it's remarkable I managed to play that character even though I'm black. Earlier in my career, when I played Rosalind in an-all male *As You Like It* for Cheek by Jowl theatre company, someone praised me by saying I was so good in the role they 'forgot' I was black. I was surprised at that one. I was playing a woman, in a modern-dress production, with hardly any set, but in order to accept the story of the play and be involved with the character they had to ignore my colour.

So here's the question I should have asked them . . . What do you assume when you see the colour of my skin?

I know they don't simply see 'me'. I have no idea what their preconceptions are. I only know that it is personal to them, it is negative and it constantly shapes everything they think. So when I step on stage to play a role, some people find it very hard to accept because they see character and colour as the same thing. Frank is fully aware of this, so much so that it leads his judgment to a protectionist stance.

Later I meet Karen Wilson and her development assistant Lillie at Kudos. Karen had lots of questions about the work I had done on the idea for a new drama series and my retelling of the plot of *We Prey*. I was expecting to have answers from her. I wanted to know what direction Kudos wanted the series to travel in, some kind of guidance as to the general path they would be interested in so that I don't work too hard heading off in the wrong direction.

I haven't done this developing thing for a while. It's good to go through the process with someone I've known for years and consider a friend.

We go through the set up I have written and the following plot line I reinvented from *We Prey* in great detail. As soon as the idea becomes procedural, something is lost. Somehow it becomes usual and standard. We keep wondering how to make the two elements work together.

As I sit on the bus on the way back to south London, I get hit by an idea. I start working out the characters arcs and realize I've found a way to make the whole thing work. Once I get home, I write the whole thing out for Karen and Lillie.

Every script, every idea, is a Rubik's Cube. The puzzle stays open in your mind for a long time even as you try to get on with other things.

Lolita   I am in a meeting with Rosa and Alan Lane of Slung Low theatre company at the Roundhouse with Marcus and his team. We are talking about *Testaments*, a theatre event I would like to put together using professionals and the young talent at the Roundhouse.

So we talk loose dates. January 2021. We talk about what we will need. The concept is that the audience start at a funeral. They all wear headphones through which they will hear a story. Each of the 'dearly departed' appears and takes a fifth of the audience on a journey through their lives and round the Roundhouse. They come together at a mid point at a party/station/airport and then at the end of the monologues they join for the interment where every member of the company and crew join a choir to sing things to a close.

With Alan's knowledge and ambitions for this kind of theatre and Rosa's vision, this could be spectacular. Anyway, Marcus and his team liked it. We will now start to move forward, thinking scale, budgets, timings and co-producers. Very exciting indeed.

Friday 2 November

Lolita I spend the whole day on an interview panel to appoint the new artistic director for Rambert. Because I'm working with the company on *Invisible Cities*, the CEO asked me to join them.

I was very honoured. I used to watch Rambert a lot when I was a student and although I was nervous as to what I might contribute, I said yes. Helen, the CEO, said that as an artist of a different discipline, I would be useful.

It is a long but very interesting day. We interview seven candidates. There were about ten of us in the room – trustees, staff, a woman from the arts council and me.

I really like what Helen is doing with Rambert. She has an eye on a current and real worldview. It is a fascinating process to be a part of and as I left, I really got a sense of the scale of the task she has in front of her: an old worldview versus a progressive one that will keep the work relevant.

Being invited to be part of change happening at a boardroom level makes me very excited to be working with her.

Sunday 4 November

Lolita I am filming today. I am playing a supporting role in *Defending the Guilty*, a new comedy drama series for TV. I am up at 5.00 am and shooting in Hatfield until 3.00 pm. The cast were very nice. The part was straightforward.

Monday 5 November

Adrian Another meeting with Callum Grant, a follow-up to his interest in Lolita's screenplay of *Red Velvet*. Much more of a general chat this time. He wants to keep track of the project. He had some ideas about how the script could be executed and was happy to talk through them.

He had a really interesting idea for reinventing the classics that Britain knows and loves so well, from Shakespeare to Chaucer including Webster and Austen. They're good ideas that we began brainstorming for bit. It set my mind thinking about modern movie adaptations of Shakespeare.

Tuesday 6 November

Adrian Meeting Marcus, Meera, Lenny, Angela Ferreira and Ade Adepitan at a pub on Whitehall. We greet each other and gather our thoughts before taking a letter to the prime minister calling for a Diversity Tax Credit to be introduced. We will hand in the letter and then be placed in front of cameras outside 10 Downing Street to explain what the tax relief is and how it would work.

We're all a little nervous. We have no idea what the media will be like. They could be quite hostile and try to force us to defend ourselves or they could be even-handed and fair in the questions, simply asking us to explain our belief in the new system.

As I'm walking with Angela toward the first interview for Sky News, I'm running through the statistics in my mind, preparing myself for the worst kind of interviewer. As I stand outside Number 10, I can feel myself becoming quite angry. Why do I have to become politicized in order to do my job? Why do I have to become a spokesperson or a campaigner for colour just so that I have the right to work? And every time I speak out, I risk losing the anonymity that benefits my work.

Year on year we have been met with excuses. The figures show us the closed-shop nature of the stories we have watched for years and yet here I am in front of another camera, another interviewer, twenty years after Treva Etienne stood outside BAFTA asking for the same things and having to answer the same questions.

I put my earpiece in ready for the interview take a breath and remind myself not to defend my position, but to make others tell me that the situation as it now stands is a fair and just indication of talent in this country. If they try to make me defend myself, or justify why we have come to this position, I will embarrass them on air.

To my surprise the interviews are full of probing thoughtful questions, which I am given the space to answer fully. We are then invited into Number 10 to have a meeting with a few of the prime minister's advisors.

Wednesday 7 November

Adrian I meet with Sharon White at Ofcom. We discuss the thinking that works against our industry being a level playing field. Sharon has long held a belief that something needs to be done and backs up her own conclusions and the statistics she is given by talking to practitioners to get a picture of what things look like 'on the shop floor'.

Later that day I attend the Mountview opening ceremony in Peckham. It's a really good evening. I see the performance facilities that the drama school brings to the area, the dance studios, practice rooms and theatres. I begin a conversation with Eddie Gower, the director of short courses, about the possibility of bringing Taekwondo to the school, not only for the local community but for the actors that are in training there.

Once the ceremony is over, I head off to catch up with some of the people I trained with at RADA over a drink.

Friday 9 November

Adrian I have been asked to do a reading as part of the ceremony at the Royal Albert Hall to mark 100 years since Armistice. The rehearsals are today, very last-minute, as the event will take place tomorrow.

Afterwards I went along to meet James Lucas at Soho House in central London. James is a writer/director who has written a pitch document for a film covering the life of James P. Beckwourth, the American mountain man. Born into slavery in 1798, he became a Black Chief of the Crow Nation after marrying a Native American Crow Nation woman, and was known as 'Bloody Arm' for his skill as a fighter. It's a good idea. The pitch doc is full of wonderful images that shine a light on his incredible story.

James is in development with Working Title but wants to pick my brains as to how he can move the project forward. As we talk, I realize that I'm not really sure why he has asked me to meet. I thought he wanted to pick my brains as a colleague but now I'm wondering as I listen to him . . . Is it to play a part? Or direct? Or maybe he wants to talk to me with a view to writing it? I'm aware I came into the meeting not knowing and therefore unsure of where the conversation was headed. I ask him straight out why he is talking to me and in what way he wants me to help. He then makes it clear that he would be happy for me to direct the project. I'm pleased but want to do what's best for the idea. So I tell him to tell Working Title that he has my firm interest. Once they know, they will do one of two things: tell him that I'm not who they had in mind and that they would rather work with someone else, or they will love the idea and want to talk further.

Either way, the fact that he met with me should galvanize them into some sort of action on the project. I tell him that my involvement is not as important to the project as the idea, and that they shouldn't sit on it for too long because he is capable of getting keen involvement elsewhere.

In reality I may not be enough to spark movement, but it's worth a try.

Lolita I am at Rambert on the South Bank today doing our first reading of *Invisible Cities*. It is an intense day, as expected. We have two brilliant actors who work extremely hard. It's a two-hander with epic descriptive language, so there was little space for them to rest. Director Leo had them read it almost four times and as they became more familiar with what they are saying, I start to hear some of the threads I have laid beneath the language.

I am pleased. I have absolutely found a dramatic arc (that needs work) and made a story with a progression, whilst staying true to Calvino's impulses. I am aware that this is an iconic book to some and an unknown quantity to others. I need to tell the story so those new to Calvino can get engaged and those who feel he is a visionary will feel fulfilled.

As the actors read the dialogue and invest it with meaning, direction, emotional intent and energy, it becomes clearer how this might work, and also where the dance, movement and digital work can sit.

I wasn't wrong when I thought I was writing a map. Everything has to be in the script so that all of these different disciplines approaching the work from different directions can all remain, quite literally, on the same page.

I go for a drink with Sam, our casting director, and the actors. It is lovely to ask them what they felt reading the piece, how it felt from the inside. They have some very good and useful ideas.

Saturday 10 November

Adrian Spent the evening chatting to my fellow readers Michael Palin and Nina Wadia at the Armistice service at the Royal Albert Hall. It is being broadcast live on TV and is an incredibly moving event. The performers, the personal accounts, the poetry and the orchestra left most of us in tears. This is a moment that gives the country an opportunity to reflect and appreciate the sacrifices of people who can sometimes be forgotten.

Lolita This evening Jasmine and I attended the performance at the Royal Albert Hall to see Adrian read a piece for the Festival for Remembrance. It is an amazing event. It is in the presence of the queen and the royal family, the prime minister and many other dignitaries.

The event is very moving. The scale of it is extraordinary, but the small human details we were given throughout the evening were superb. They marked and remembered veterans of all ages, the animals who served on the battlefields, the hospitals that cared for the injured, the parents of those lost, the First World War, Second World War, Afghanistan, the Falklands, the soldiers of empire who lost their lives. It presented us with the enormous sacrifices made in violent wars fought to try and build peace. Tom Jones, Bryn Terfel, Sheridan Smith, Adrian, Michael Palin and Nina Wadia performed and presented. I am so glad to have had the opportunity to attend.

You can get lost in the self-importance of your own work sometimes, and to see what so many have sacrificed for the safety of others was very humbling indeed. The veterans were amazing, marching proudly in their eighties and nineties alongside their teenage modern counterparts. I researched The Royal British Legion briefly for a piece I wanted to write for TV and they do phenomenal work. It was a brief glimpse into an essential community.

Sunday 11 November

Adrian   Had a late night after the event yesterday and I'm up early for an interview on Talk Radio regarding the Diversity Tax Relief. I'm shattered but manage to have a good chat with the interviewers. Some very good questions were asked, which gave me the chance to explain the idea in more detail.

Thursday 15 November

Lolita   I finish my first draft of *Politically Correct* and send it off to Hedda at Fiery Angel. I always call my first draft a crayon drawing where I map out the basics – characters, story arc, locations. It's broad but the first baby steps.

Saturday 17 November

Lolita   I am in auditions for *Pi* with director Max. We're in Fulham and puppet and movement director Finn is putting actors through a movement session and basic puppet skills before we briefly hear the actors read scenes. We are seeing thirty-six actors today and saw the same number yesterday. We're looking for a very specific skill set, so it's a very wide and diverse casting process.

It's interesting seeing how the actors move and how open they are to working as an ensemble.

After these sessions, we will have recalls. It's a long and detailed process.

Monday 19 November

Lolita   I am at the Mayfair Hotel to meet Basil and Adrian of Handspring Puppet Company – they made the puppets for *War Horse*. I have been asked to adapt *The Elephant Whisperer*, an autobiographical book about a game-reserve conservationist and a herd of wild elephants.

The book is a good basis from which to tell a story, but this would be a big adaptation and I am unsure about taking on another large project. But when I meet Basil and Adrian, I really like the way they speak about their approach to their work. It's infectious and makes me keen to do this.

Then I have a meeting with director Leo about *Invisible Cities*. We speak about the reading and I get his notes for the next draft. This project melts my mind a little. His thoughts include internal notes for the characters but also practical decisions for moving certain sections of dialogue in order to facilitate the design. The book is about Venice and so the progression of water through the piece has been a design idea from the beginning. Leo wants it to be introduced and then accumulate so that by the end of the performance, the space is flooded. But of course I have to work out what this means emotionally. During our meeting I get more of a sense of what the other elements of the performance are going to be.

Once I'm at home, I disappear into my office and call Rick at Chicago Shakespeare Theater (CST). Last year CST did a production of *Red Velvet*. I went out there to see it and to do a few talks. But seventeen years ago in 2001, CST hosted Adrian playing *Hamlet* in Peter Brook's company. I had just had our first child and went out there with an eight-week-old baby. The artistic director of CST, Barbara Gaines, looked after me and baby Lila so well I never forgot it, and when Rick contacted me about doing *Red Velvet* there I was really thrilled. Rick has now connected me with the producer for *The Elephant Whisperer*, so I have a few questions for him about what this might be before I make my decision.

Tuesday 20 November

Adrian   Attending an informal gathering of people who work in the creative sector invited by the mayor of London, Sadiq Khan. In his short address, he says that the reason for the evening is because he wants to acknowledge the influence the performing arts industry has on London in terms of the money it brings in, not only to the capital but also the entire country. For every pound spent on the arts, the return the country gets outstrips every other industry.

He thanks us for being a part of that and encourages us to keep creating, adding that wherever possible he would champion a creative industry that was vibrant, inclusive and continued to grow at such an exponential rate. I spend the evening brainstorming and chatting with Marcus Davey, Lenny Henry, Ben Okri and many other colleagues there.

Of course, the group of people I'm with are the loudest, and the last to leave.

Thursday 22 November

Lolita   I meet Max and Simon this afternoon and Jack Bradley, who is giving me some dramaturgical help on *Pi*. It is a good session. I am generally wary of script editors, having worked with one a few years ago on a film I was writing. She was extremely experienced and had strong ideas, but after a while of working with her I realized she was gently eroding my confidence. She implied that she should help me deconstruct the script and do a rewrite, that my own impulses were irrelevant compared to her expertise. It became extremely uncomfortable and I extracted myself from the situation. I now know that with creative work in any field, you must really choose carefully who you work with. A voice of self-interest at the delicate beginning of an idea can crush your intentions and your confidence. It's a very subtle thing.

I'm very pleased to find that this session with Jack Bradley is the opposite. He asks questions that help me gain a new overview of the piece.

Afterwards Max and I go to meet Andrew T. Mackay, a potential composer for *Pi*. He is very good and has the right understanding of Eastern and Western musical traditions in his work. It is a good meeting. We offer him the job. I hope he does it.

Thursday 29 November

Adrian   A week ago I got a play sent through to my agent from Hampstead Theatre called *Cost Of Living*. It's a Pulitzer Prize winner by Martyna Majok.

As soon as I began to read the play, I was hooked. It's full of very simple realistic dialogue, broken sentences revealing hidden vulnerabilities. The play takes place in present-day New Jersey and has, only four characters, two of whom are wheelchair users. It is so sparse, I am really intrigued. The run is not as long I would usually do in the theatre; it's basically two months.

Today I'm off to meet Edward Hall, the play's director, for lunch to discuss it. Edward is warm, charming and completely honest with every response to my questions. There's no pretence. He is passionate about the project and the more we talk, the more I see just how much painful detail the writer has placed into the lives of these characters. No one could write what she has written without personal knowledge of a life with disability and care workers.

It would be completely different to anything I have done before. Should I accept?

Lolita   I spend the week redrafting *Invisible Cities*. I am tightening the relationship between Kublai Khan and Marco Polo, but also trying to fit the design ideas into the story. Leo wants a high-octane opening – a two-minute projection event to start the evening off. That's a pretty wide canvas to be set as a writer. So to think of something that fulfils that feeling, but adds to my story, is challenging.

All hail the internet, where I can travel the world from the comfort of my office. I look up the very loose journey from Venice to Shangdu, Kublai Khan's palace, and then looked up natural phenomena along the way. I cheat a little – I thought the Northern Lights would be spectacular, as would ice flow and then mountains. Anyway I have offered a two-minute high-octane natural projection moment at the beginning of the piece that will help detail an essential journey one of the characters would have to make at the start.

I also have to keep an eye on the movement of water throughout the piece. We have a moment of a barge on a river. At the end of the piece, Leo wants the whole space flooded. He also suggested a water curtain, so I have inserted that into a new set needed for a sacred space because water is soothing. Then I've punctuated the story with a gradual need for water till we can achieve Leo's vision of a flood at the end.

Anyway, all this is the long way to say that I have finished the next draft and sent it to everyone.

Saturday 1 December

Lolita We have been auditioning for *Pi* for the last two days. It's been intense but very good. Max and I have found some really strong contenders. We will offer another four or five roles next week. It's great to see who we can get and to put faces to the roles. Now it's fingers crossed that they accept. Then it's on to the next audition. There are thirteen actors to cast.

Wednesday 5 December

Adrian It's the ICAP trading day event in the City. Every year for the past twenty-five years, ICAP has given 100 per cent of its commissions on one day's trading to chosen charities. They have made £4.5 million for charity so far and the event happens all over the world. I'm going along as a representative of Body & Soul, which the trading teams have chosen as one of the charities that will benefit from their donations this year.

I go from floor to floor through a large bank in the City watching the teams of traders who are dressed as the Spice Girls, Marvel superheroes, dinosaurs and Disney characters whilst carrying out their deals. I get on the phone a few times to close a few of them, crack jokes, take selfies and generally have fun with the staff. The Body & Soul team that are also present have such heart. They talk about how much they might raise for the families that rely on them. I leave, dismissing their thanks and trying to thank *them* for all the work they do.

I jump in a car and get myself over to Mountview Theatre School in Peckham, where I have a meeting with Eddie Gower, the short courses director about how martial arts might be useful to the acting students. Stage fighting is much the same on stage as it has always been but on-screen, actors are often asked to fight as though they have some kind of previous training. I think a martial arts system in a drama school will be good for the students. It will increase their confidence, balance, timing and general physical awareness as they go through their course. The quality of the teacher is paramount to this. Eddie likes the idea and we agree to chat further.

Even though Mountview is on my doorstep, I know that the commitment needed to turn up regularly every week as a teacher is something I cannot give.

An hour has passed and it's time for me to go into a Q&A with the acting students. I'm asked if it can be recorded for the benefit of the students who can't be present. At first I agree but then change my mind. I ask if all recording devices can be turned off. The students put away their phones and promise me that what is said will be kept completely private and suddenly the energy and focus changes in the room. They are all incredibly present, something that technology can stop us being, and this affords me the opportunity to be very honest. I speak about my upbringing, my approach to the work, the bad decisions I've made and the one's that seem to have worked. We have a good conversation about Othello, Rosalind, Hamlet and playing Shakespeare in general.

Lolita   I am two days into another workshop on *Pi*. This is smaller. We are in a rehearsal room in Pimlico – me, Max and four actors who have come in to help. They are not part of the cast but have kindly agreed to help us work through the latest draft of the play. It is dense work. The structure of the play is now pretty good, but it's the internal machinations of the scenes and how each moment informs the next and pushes the story on that needs work. I am making reams of notes because the technical ideas I need to incorporate are very precise.

I am finding it very good work, but hard to keep a hold of the whole piece. I have so many versions in my head now – I can't remember which bits have stayed in this draft and which are gone. It will all make sense in the end. I think that's why I make so many notes – a map for myself when I navigate them afterwards.

We are also squeezing in auditions around this workshop. Max and I meet a little earlier in the morning to audition someone and spend our lunch break seeing actors too.

Sunday 9 December

Lolita   The last day of this workshop on *Pi*. Having done three days with four actors, we are now working with four actor puppeteers, Finn the puppet and movement director, and several prototype puppets. It's really thought-provoking to see how the puppets need space and the writing needs a different rhythm to make them work. It's also interesting being in the room where the actors are constantly offering up ideas and interpretations. Finn is adding detail and logic to the animals and their relationship with *Pi*. Max is moving through each scene with an eye on the wider story and finally, I work to change intentions behind the words so that they suit everyone. I am really enjoying this level of collaboration.

Actors have slowly been accepting our offers. A couple more actors accepted the job and joined the cast today – it's starting to take shape.

Monday 10 December

Adrian   *Mary Queen of Scots* press junket all day. I'm in and out of hotel rooms talking to journalists about the film. Some interviews chat about the movie, others try to be friendly and light in order to blindside you with personal questions in the hope that even your evasive answer will get them extra column inches. I always find this annoying but of course never ever show it and find the best response is to be honest and let them know what I won't talk about. Tina, our manager and publicist, is present. She sits behind the interviewer and with a look or a nod she lets me know whether I should continue or she will sometimes close down the question for me so that I don't have to do or say anything negative and printable.

This is followed by the red-carpet premiere for the film in Leicester Square. It was good to see the film again on the big screen. Josie Rourke, our director, mentions that she would like to chat to me about an idea she has for her final show as artistic director at the Donmar Warehouse.

Monday 17 December

Lolita   I am in a reading of *Invisible Cities*. This is the third draft. We are back at Rambert with director Leo, casting director Sam and two new actors.

As I listen to them read, I am struck by the fact that the narrative doesn't fully work yet, but I am pleased to have carved out a story where there was none and given character where there wasn't any. I know that is the way of the writer/adapter – to translate the narrative into a dramatic story, but this one has been particularly challenging.

By the end, I was a little punch-drunk. It's dense material that will ultimately be expanded by dance and projection, but just hearing the words in this way is a bit full on.

After the reading, we chat about casting. There are only two actors needed, but the skill set is very particular and it is going to be a challenge finding actors who will suit all the producers involved. We will get there, but I do get impatient with the time it is taking.

This is my last day of work before Christmas. I have a few ends to tie up but no more writing until January. I feel like I am on the cusp of getting a better work/life balance. It also means that while the kids are off school/college, I can be around and less preoccupied.

Creative work takes up so much headspace. There's the time that you are actually doing it, but then there is the planning, thought and all of the half-realized ideas that continue to permeate no matter where you are. With all these writing projects and the intermittent acting jobs, half of my brain always seems to be preoccupied. It is very nice to truly stop and be present for our girls.

Tuesday 18 December

Adrian   Today is the first day of rehearsals for *Cost of Living* at Hampstead Theatre. After a couple of days of deliberating, I went with my gut and signed on to the project.

The company are great. Director Edward Hall has decided that he wants to do four days' work before Christmas. We start with a read-through and a chat about the characters and the world of the play. Katy Sullivan is an American actor and has done the play before. She has had three award nominations for all three productions where she played the character of 'Ani' in Williamstown, New York and LA. In fact, after her final performance in LA she went to her dressing room where her bags were already packed to come to London and start rehearsals with us. I wonder how open she will be to exploring the role again with a different actor playing her husband.

We read, work and talk, I'm all ears as Jack Hunter, who has cerebral palsy, and Katy, who was born without legs below the knee, tell us how people sometimes react to their disability. Giggling as they recount moments where people have gone into disability-panic, overcompensating for their reactions to seeing them.

Wednesday 19 December

Lolita   I am on the phone to Annette, who is producing *The Elephant Whisperer*. My contract is not completed yet, but I am already starting to think of how to tackle the piece and needed to speak to her. I tell her I won't be able to write anything until September and she is happy with that. To me it sounds a long way away, but I know I have a lot of research and thinking to do in this interim. The writing will be relatively quick – six weeks for a first draft.

We have a great chat about our initial ideas. She is very warm on the phone and I start to feel a buzz and get excited. This could be a wonderful project. She wants to give me the time to find the story, which is reassuring. It's a great chat of ideas and directions and it is my last bit of work this year. It is a very satisfying way to finish 2018.

Friday 4 January 2019

Lolita   I am having my first meeting of the New Year. I won't start working properly until next week. I am having coffee with Tim Levy, a British producer, who has returned here after many years in New York. Whilst there, he helped produce the National Theatre's shows in America – including *War Horse*, so he has obviously worked with Basil and Adrian of Handspring before. I am here to talk about *The Elephant Whisperer*, but also to get to know him and vice versa. I see that writing and producing is a very long game and ultimately you want to know that you will have a fruitful and good time while working together for years.

He is interested in perhaps coming on board for this – although he will wait for the first draft in October. I like him a lot and his skill set is impressive, so fingers crossed.

I really enjoy being able to build a project from the ground up. I am aware that I have to not overstep my role in the process but working with those who can embrace all my skills is very pleasing.

Tuesday 8 January

Adrian   Spend the morning in rehearsals for *Cost of Living*. They are going well. Even though Katy Sullivan has played the part so many times, she is very open to rediscovering moments on stage with me, the third actor playing her husband in this play.

I'm really enjoying the opportunity to pull back while I play this intimate four-hander that Martyna Majok has written so succinctly. We are very lucky to have Martyna in the room with us as we gently put the play into the space and work out what we might do. Not a word on the page can be wasted and anything extra has been cut. She has written a very lean script.

In the afternoon I rush over to meet Lenny Henry, Marcus Ryder, Angela Ferreira and Pat Younge. We have a meeting with the DCMS (Department for Digital, Culture, Media and Sport) and the Treasury to put our case forward for a Diversity Tax Credit. A representative of the BFI is there, as they have very recently rolled out a set of rules to increase the diversity of the films that they will consider for funding. It is clear that these departments are considering the idea seriously. If a tax credit will spark an increase in production, it will lead to increased revenue and who doesn't want that? We'll see where we get with this. Brexit is keeping everyone on their toes and during this period of dire uncertainty people in all major government departments seem to be more concerned with sustaining current systems rather than implementing new ones. But now that this idea is on the table, it has to be formally looked at.

Wednesday 9 January

Lolita   I am in a meeting with director Leo Warner, getting my notes on the reading of the last draft of *Invisible Cities* we did last year. He has been thinking a lot about this over Christmas as I see from his notes.

He opens a roll of paper the size of my dining table (which seats eight people), on which he has deconstructed the script and moved scenes around. He is working on a logic of his own.

I find Calvino hard. This book gives you much space to ponder what is going on. There is little logic and much open thought. So my battle writing it has been to try and make it active and forward moving when the book is contrary to that – it is languid and philosophical – the antithesis to what theatre demands. I have found my own logic to the story. But now Leo is thinking how to realize this story in physical form – with dancers and projection. So he needs his logic.

When he opened the chart of notes I wasn't sure where to start, but he just talked for two hours and slowly it made sense. What's great is that he describes some of the images he and designer Jenny are starting to form and it really helps my thoughts for story. This is the bit I love – the collaboration and combining of ideas and disciplines. This is why I took this job. It's also really interesting because, whilst I am thinking story, arc, character, progression, feeling etc., he thinks in shapes and spatial ideas.

Leo and I spend a good couple of hours deconstructing his ideas and at the end of it I think neither of us is sure of the way forward. Thankfully he gives me the giant spreadsheet and I know, from experience, that I just need to follow the first idea and then the second and it will reveal itself. Simple, isn't it, in the end – one step in front of the other and you get where you're going.

Thursday 10 January

Lolita I am at Longcross Studios having a meeting with Ken Branagh about the film of *Red Velvet*. I finished this draft last July, but he has been incredibly busy and unable to meet until now. We sit in his bright, spacious office and he is taking me through his ideas for the next draft. They're great – tightening and directing the action to be more uncertain, more edgy, better to watch.

I am reminded of him coming to our house some twenty years ago and giving me detailed notes on a film treatment I had written about Ira. I was a young actress then, starting to write and he took me very seriously and treated my work then with detail and respect. His encouragement back then has stayed with me down the years.

Amazing to be here again but now *Red Velvet* has been realized, Ira Aldridge is in the public consciousness again and I have written the film.

I have reintroduced Edmund Kean, thought to be the greatest actor of his generation in the early nineteenth century, a complex and fascinating character. It's been very satisfying to reinstate him in the film and to write him for Ken to play should or when *Red Velvet* gets made.

I come out of this meeting tired but excited. I can feel I am getting closer to a good script.

Friday 18 January

Adrian   *Cost of Living* rehearsals. This character is quite different to any I have tackled before, and I can feel myself take a few days to climb down from an energy that is used to performing large spaces in order to perform for the house at Hampstead, playing a man who hides his emotions.

Acting requires you to dig into human behaviour in order to form an understanding of character. The knowledge you gain is conscious. It stays in the front of your mind. The task in performance is to hide all of that knowledge so that speech and movement look unconscious.

My character is Eddie Torres, a recovering alcoholic whose sensitivity to the world around him is buried in a place he never articulates. It is the complete opposite of Shakespeare in its form of expression. For Eddie, everything he doesn't say is the most important thing on his mind. The audience reads the needs of the people in this play because they do and say almost the opposite of what they need and want.

The play starts with me delivering a fifteen-minute monologue. I learned most of it before rehearsals started (no point leaving the task of learning it hanging round my neck while trying to get on with other scenes). As I deliver it, Edward Hall and I talk about how much to bury and how much to reveal. Edward has a keen eye; I have never worked with him before, but during these crucial one-on-one moments in the rehearsal room I begin to trust him implicitly as he guides me through elements that will be too clear for the audience and seem 'acted' and elements that are too hidden and will therefore be lost. The monologue is my map through my character's persona as he deals with his pain and guilt.

Edward is a great guide. I'm very glad I took this job.

Mary Queen of Scots gets its cinema release today. I wonder how it will do.

Wednesday 23 January

Adrian The rehearsals flew by. I'm now at the technical rehearsal for *Cost of Living*. The tech always offers me a curious moment to fully connect with the job I have to do. At no other time am I afforded minutes on stage, with the props, the lighting, and the faces of the other actors in stillness. A time where I don't speak and am required to do nothing but follow the deputy stage manager's cues incorporating set, props, lighting and sound. It provides hours where I'm left alone and can attach my belief to the situation around me a little deeper than I could in the rehearsal room. My character has a blanket that belongs to my dead wife. I know that it is a necessary and important part of my journey with her and on stage during the tech is the only time I have to be with that prop, to invest it with the reality that I need from it during performance.

As the stage manager relays commands and questions from Edward to the lighting desk, I stare at the blanket and imagine different scenarios linked to the life Ani (my deceased wife) and I have lived. I briefly imagine the moment she bought it. The times I've wrapped it around her shoulders when she has been cold or too drunk to make it to our bed. Passed out. Helpless. I've always been there, keeping her warm, making sure she's ok. It becomes an emblem of my care and love for her.

Only in my mind, though. Just in my mind. I don't tell the director or the actress playing my wife. This is for me. It's the invented memory that I place into my performance that sustains me on a long run. So many times during the shows that I have done, my mind has wandered off onto other things and been caught and pulled back into the life of the play by the imagined life of an inanimate object.

Thursday 24 January

Lolita I am doing an acting job for Netflix in Madrid. The cast is strong, the piece is really interesting and well written. I love being an actor in the middle of writing – there is a freedom and play in acting. You need to follow your emotional instincts and distil what you feel into the character you're playing. Writing is very empowering but feels like a huge responsibility sometimes.

This series is called *Criminal*. I'm just in one episode. It's intense filming, all set inside a police investigation room. It's an hour of old-school, well-written, strongly acted drama. The cast and crew were really nice and welcoming. It's a British cast and a mainly Spanish crew, but the director, writer and director of photography are Brits too. I'm present all the time throughout the episode, but as the solicitor of the suspect, played by David Tennant, I say very little. So in truth I am a little restless.

I took this job because the script is really good and it is rare these days to get something this strong. I also thought that, with all these scripts in my own head, not having too many lines would be good. I'd have much screen time and less stress. But actually I am frustrated by it. I have cleared this week to focus on the acting so I am not writing at all. I am doing a little reading, but with no deadline. So it is interesting being here because I realize I need more. If I make the space for acting, I have to get more from it. Be more invested, have the challenge.

Anyway being in Madrid is a real treat. I have noticed there is a different feel amongst women here, an appreciation of all ages and types of woman. When I visited the cathedral, I was very struck how central women were in the stained glass windows, the sculpture. It is rare to see. In fact I can't remember feeling that before. This feels like a strongly female-centric country.

Friday 25 January

Adrian Josie Rourke's idea for her final show at the Donmar Warehouse is to do the musical *Sweet Charity*.

There are lots of iconic songs in this piece by Cy Coleman, Dorothy Fields and Neil Simon; one of them is 'The Rhythm of Life', originally sung in the film version by Sammy Davis Jr. Josie has an idea about the song that she hopes will work. She believes that because that song is delivered by a character that has no other part in the show, Josie wants to direct it with a different actor coming in to perform 'The Rhythm of Life' every week. Actors who, for the most part, have some sort of performance history with the Donmar. The actor playing Big Daddy Brubeck would change so often that the audience would have no idea who was coming out to sing at that moment.

She asks me if I would kick the whole thing off by delivering the song in the previews, then the opening night, and carry on for a week or two.

I think about it for about half a second before I say yes. What a great idea.

Wednesday 31 January

Lolita I am in auditions for *Invisible Cities* today at Rambert on the South Bank. In the morning director Leo and casting director Sam and I see a few actors for the role of Marco Polo. As we gear up to production the skill set of this role is very specific – a strong actor and text-speaker, with strong physical ability. He has to be able to join the dancers but not dance. We saw an extremely diverse group of actors.

The afternoon was spent in a dance studio with Rambert artistic director, Benoit, and dancer Matthew. They put a recall selection of actors through some movement paces for a couple of hours. They are very open to their different abilities in the room, but it's demanding and rigorous. Hats off to the actors involved – they threw themselves into it.

So fascinating to watch Benoit at work. His instructions are clear, precise and generous, but his expectation is that it is done well. That's the difference between actors and dancers – dancers have to strive for absolute excellence now because otherwise you can't be in the room. It is very exciting to watch another discipline at such a top level at work.

When I was at RADA my friend worked in the offices at Rambert, so I went to see their work a lot. Being in this room now as one of the creative team was not a path I ever imagined taking. There is an absolute diversity of talent, type of person and skills in this room.

I have also joined another dance project. Kate Prince, the artistic director of ZooNation, a hip-hop company I have followed for years with great admiration, has asked me to be the dramaturg on her next show, *Message in a Bottle*. It's a dance show based on the music of The Police and Sting, and is about refugees. I am thrilled to be a part of that, too. I am not sure how this has come about but I have always loved dance – I have been an uninformed watcher. To be in the room now, spinning story around movement, is opening my mind. I am feeling very energized by my work.

Adrian   Opening night for *Cost of Living* at Hampstead. Even though we had done four previews to prepare ourselves, the opening night is always nerve-wracking as it is the moment you feel you are judged. Publicly.

The lights go down and I walk out on stage to begin a fifteen-minute monologue full of broken thoughts, unfinished sentences and repetitions. My heart is in my mouth as I approach the audience.

At Q&As I am often asked by people for tips on how to get over the nerves they feel onstage. How can they get rid of them? I tell them not to be fooled. The people they admire haven't got over their nerves either. They just act like they have. If a person is not nervous to some degree before going out on stage and delivering more than an hour of intricate live performance, then there's something wrong with them, or what they deliver. Nerves are a normal human reaction to that kind of situation. It means we care about what we do, how we may appear and what we want the audience to understand. The only way to deal with nerves is to accept them. Know that they are real and they are helping to sharpen every sense in your body. The only thing you can do is find ways to relax your body as much as possible. Being unrelaxed and being nervous are not quite the same thing.

I place my stool down, pick up my glass of water and say Eddie's first thought. Am I nervous . . . YES!

The evening goes well. Relieved, we all celebrate in the bar afterwards. People approach Jack Hunter and Katy Sullivan, thanking them for opening their eyes and showing them a glimpse of what the world looks like when you use a wheelchair. 'Thanking them' may sound a bit strong, but Martyna's play genuinely has that effect. Others, at the other end of that understanding, tell me stories of having cared for loved ones who were wheelchair users, commenting on the detail and sincerity in the play. They tell me it is something they never see on stage and they were moved by the experience. I point them over to Martyna Majok and say they should tell her.

Friday 8 February

Lolita   I am in Birmingham at St Mary's Church in Harborne for the funeral of my drama teacher, Miss Maureen Stack. There are other old girls here and a handful of teachers from school. I left thirty-two years ago. It's a lovely service and some of the hymns are the ones I know from my days at Holy Child School in Edgbaston. Being in a Catholic church always reminds me of those days – how I railed and fought against the tradition and ceremony back then and now it feels familiar and comforting. I am not Catholic.

Miss Stack was incredibly glamorous and an extrovert when I was an awkward twelve-year-old, just returning from a year of living in India. She was bleach blonde, slim and shapely, wore tight-fitting, eye-catching dresses and was always tottering around on stiletto heels. She flirted shamelessly with everyone's dad but was a staunch Catholic and a true-blue Conservative. She was the absolute opposite of me, then and now. *But* she was the one who saw I was good at drama. She encouraged me to act and write from the start. I did all my LAMDA medals in acting, speaking and mime with her. She was at every public-speaking competition I did and celebrated every win. When I was on local TV with one of my speeches, she was with me and when I was in the local paper, she was there too. She was the one who gave me the application for RADA and said 'why not try?', and she was the one who squealed with delight when I got in.

We made contact after many years this Christmas and were going to meet when she came to see *Pi* and *Invisible Cities* in the summer. She died unexpectedly and suddenly. She was only sixty-eight.

I am struck by how important people come quietly, guide you and let you fly, expecting nothing. She was so important in building my confidence and showing me the way to this life I have now. I only saw her a handful of times after I left school but her input and influence were always felt. I told her that when I last saw her almost ten years ago. She often asked me to call her Maureen, but for me, she will always and forever be the blonde bombshell that was Miss Stack. RIP.

Tuesday 12 February

Adrian   Mike Bartlett is in to see the show tonight. I first worked with Mike on a three-parter he wrote for ITV called *Trauma*. He is a fantastic writer to work for, meticulous, thoughtful and collaborative. He has written a six-parter for the BBC called *Life*, which will be produced by the same team that did *Doctor Foster*. It's a great script and there is a strong wish for me to play one of the roles in the piece, but I have to wait and see what happens with a possible second series of *The Rook*, as the first series hasn't aired yet.

Friday 15 February

Lolita   I am handing in the rehearsal draft of *Invisible Cities* today. Big sigh of relief. It required restructuring, tightening and incorporating design elements. Holding the design of the space in my mind with the inspiration of images from the mood board is a very different way to work for me. But I have enjoyed it. I was feeling pressured by not just the time constraints, but also the split in my mind between acting and writing. We've also cast *Invisible Cities*, which is really great. Danny Sapani, who I imagined when I wrote it, is doing it. And a young actor called Matthew Leonhart.

I can now move onto the next. I am refreshing the pitches for three-part television drama *Rolling Over*, the murder story that my dad was involved in, so that producer Kate Bartlett can try again. I have worked on this story for twenty years. It has been a single film, a three-parter for the BBC, a three-parter for ITV. I've had suggestions to turn it into a play. Everyone loves the story, but no one commissions it. Returning to this pitch (again!) the characters are very familiar but the pitch felt flabby – too many extra words, not succinct enough. I am writing so much I'm getting better at saying what I mean.

Little bits of acting are also bubbling along. I read a story for BBC Radio 4 earlier this week and I may do a voice over for two documentaries about India for the BFI in March.

Friday 21 February

Adrian   Shaun Dooley, an actor I worked with on an episode of *Hustle*, has been back in touch about an idea that he and his wife Polly had.

Their company, 20four7 Films, is going to work with the charity Children In Need and produce an album of artists doing cover versions of some of their favourite songs.

The whole thing would be filmed for a documentary to go out on 31 October, with the album hopefully raising some money for the charity by around 10 November, when the annual Children in Need show is broadcast on the BBC.

It's a good idea for a very good cause. I've already told him I'd like to be involved and the song I'd like to sing. He thinks things will happen possibly around June depending on my availability. I let him know I'll be waiting and start listening to my chosen song, 'I Wish' by Stevie Wonder, to see what I could do with it in a cover version.

Monday 25 February

Lolita   I am back working on *Red Velvet* the film. At last, I have a space of two weeks to do it. Ken Branagh's notes for the next draft of the film of *Red Velvet* are all about upping the stakes, not being complacent and tightening the dialogue. I know these characters like old friends so making them say other things feels nice. It is enjoyable working on it again. It is finished and I've sent it to Ken.

I am also researching *The Elephant Whisperer* and trawling through the book to try and find the bones of the story. It's coming.

I am simultaneously arranging Adrian's and my fiftieth birthday party for mid-March, finding wine, cakes, marquees and caterers in the gaps. Lila turns eighteen next weekend (I can't quite believe it) and is having a party. Jasmine turns fifteen in three weeks' time and she will have a smaller gathering. All of it takes thought and planning. I feel my age in a good way – and bad. The good way is that I am starting to care less about what is thought of me and just going for what I want. The bad way is being tired and so stiff!

Thursday 7 March

Lolita　I'm going to the launch of the Manchester International Festival (MIF). I travel up on the train and manage to do a bit of work. I became a trustee for the Royal Victoria Hall Foundation (RVHF) earlier this year. My task as trustee is to form an opinion of theatre companies applying for a grant. This is my first time assessing and I read two reports on the train. Really interesting to read the reports and judge whether they should get the grant. I remember filling out applications like these when I was in my twenties, and Adrian and I started Ensemble Theatre Company.

I also reread *Invisible Cities* to re-engage with my adaptation. I have been working on *Politically Correct* the last week, so it was good to switch focus.

I am in a cab going to the announcement. There are many artists and investors here. In a huge concert venue they have erected what looks like a boxing ring around which all press and audience will stand. Then as John McGrath, artistic director of MIF, announces each project in this epic two weeks of theatre, dance, art and performance, each artist will go up and speak for a couple of minutes. I am with director Leo and Benoit, artistic director of Rambert.

The programme is vast and eclectic – Yoko Ono, Idris Elba, Maxine Peake, Skepta, us and many more. Our announcement goes well. We talk to the press afterwards: at last I can speak publicly about this.

Back to London on the train with Karl, who is investing in *Invisible Cities* and Leo. Very nice way to come back to London. I am really enjoying this collaboration. It's so big, bold and fearless. It breaks all rules.

Saturday 9 March

Adrian　Last performance of *Cost of Living* at Hampstead today. As I go through each moment, I quietly tell myself 'I'll never do that again'. Starting with the monologue, this long, detailed, complicated and revealing monologue. I've been reciting it two or three times a day now for the past six weeks. I'm so glad I went into rehearsal with most of it learned, not only because it saves time and gives you the space to concentrate on other aspects of the play, but because it's always a good idea to tackle the biggest problems first.

Watching directors Declan Donnellan and Peter Brook in rehearsal, they both played with the most difficult ideas that the plays put forward first. Once they had that ground semi-worked out, it gave them a template for the way in which the rest of the story might take place.

With Declan, for *As You Like It*, we improvised to establish the court with elements of bullying and status work. This helped for the wrestling scene and the world Rosalind had to escape from. With Peter, he and I sat together for a week before any of the other actors were called, just going through Hamlet's soliloquies, working on the changes in thought at each point in the play. Solving these problems early became a methodology for the look and feel of the production.

Learning the soliloquies for Hamlet and the monologue for Eddie also freed up space for me to work on other things rather than getting those lines under my belt.

It's a funny process, letting go of the emotional triggers that you have built up over months in one night. Unpeeling the imagined layers of a life you've invented. As I am making my way through the fifteen-minute monologue at the beginning of the play, I can feel myself letting go of the rules and words that took up all that space in my mind.

By the time we finish the show, I can see the other actors empty themselves of the work, too. The work isn't outside of ourselves. It is inside and it sits there until the job is done.

The way this play deals with people and their generalized responses to those who have a disability is exceptional. I am so glad I said yes to this project.

Saturday 16 March

Lolita   Today is Adrian and my joint fiftieth birthday party.

We're celebrating at home with a marquee in the garden and caterers. We have 140 people coming, people that cross our lives – family, friends, colleagues. It has taken a lot of planning – not unlike our wedding.

I found caterers who are doing some great Caribbean food and we've bought loads of drinks. All of our friends and family are here. I was nervous before, because it felt a bit too much. We both regularly avoid any attention we get in our private life, so to instigate a party where we are the centre of attention feels wrong. But this is us. Not our public personas. This is a celebration with those nearest and dearest to us. We had family, school friends, people we trained with, people we've worked with in the past and will do in the future, our kids with their friends, mum friends, neighbours. It was absolutely ace, so good that, even though we were officially warned to keep the music down, the party finished at around 3.00 am.

Tuesday 19 March

Adrian   Sean Foley has just been announced as the new artistic director of Birmingham Rep. Lolita worked with him on *Hamlet* with Ken Branagh and Tom Hiddleston. Sean is excited at the opportunity his new position offers, he has lots of plans and has approached Lolita and me to see if we, as Brummies, would like to do anything at the theatre.

He's very effusive, complimentary and makes us feel as though anything is possible. Although Sean speaks of the Birmingham audience with great passion, citing the diaspora and the great countrywide reputation the Rep once had years ago, I don't immediately feel as though anything would be a good fit for me there. There's too much I'm trying to get done on screen or on stage in London. But I'm more than happy to meet up and see what might inspire us.

After a brief chat with Lolita she mentions *Calmer*, the play she wrote after *Red Velvet*. I think it's a great piece and has a leading role that she is perfect for. Ever the producer – she really should run a building – she puts forward the idea of her writing and playing a lead role with me as director. I wonder if Sean will go for it.

Lolita sends him the play.

Friday 22 March

Lolita   I am in the final workshop for *Pi*. We are midway through two weeks of work. We've worked this week on script and next week will be staging, working out how to put four wild animals, a boy, a boat and fish on stage all at once and make it a clear story.

The design team, led by Tim Hatley, have built a prototype boat in the rehearsal room that makes this feel very real.

It is a week of testing the script and trying to tell the story well, given all the different needs and talents in the room. It is in equal parts exhilarating and exhausting. So many ideas are coming at me that need solutions, that by the end of the day I cannot think straight. Plus I am ill. An offshoot from the rigorous writing schedule I have been under and drinking too much at our party.

It is very sobering seeing the design of the set and puppets and the detail that goes into every consideration of this piece that starts with the script. That is what we are all working with. When it doesn't work, they look at me. It's a huge responsibility. Anyway all I can do is take the firm hand of director Max, who is giving me many possibilities and find enough silence in my head to make a decision about what serves the story.

This process is carving me into a better artist.

Friday 29 March

Lolita I am in the last day of the last *Pi* workshop. It has been an important couple of weeks. We have tested the script and most of the staging – puppets, boat, people.

I have rewritten most of the script and today we are reading it to invited guests from Sheffield, some of the creatives, producer Simon and Katie, my literary agent.

The reading goes well I think, but I can't tell as I'm too immersed in the mechanics of the story.

Caroline, who is making the puppets with Nick, has a lovely reaction. She gives me a big hug, says she never got the book as a teenager and so hasn't read the scripts at all. But hearing this, she was so moved and teary. That was really wonderful.

We are at the pub after it all. These are such nice people and I am delighted that this is some of our cast. Max has done such a good job in guiding me and the team to tell the story well. His clarity of thought and purpose is invaluable in a story which thinks of existential matters. It is easy not to travel dramatically and just chat, but Max keeps the whole thing on course with good humour and intent.

Next stop is rehearsals in under two months. That's sobering. It will be a five-week rehearsal but there will be so much to do. I think we're almost ready.

This is going to be an unusual show – a family piece that will hopefully have you travelling far within it. It's a sad but positive story and with all the design, video projection, music, puppets, acting, sound, it will hopefully be a feast.

Today we heard back from Sean Foley at Birmingham Rep. He really likes *Calmer*. He would like me to work on it, with him producing it at the Rep and Adrian directing. I love this play. For me, it discusses so many pertinent issues. It has been difficult to get this play on but now it has a home and how wonderful that it's Birmingham Rep. I have never worked there in my thirty-year career – it feels right.

Saturday 30 March

Adrian   Lolita and I are very excited about Sean's response to *Calmer*. We begin talking about the play, the possible design for the theatre it would be in, how it might be realized, and the elements we will need in the actors that might do it with us. It's only when I see Lolita politely nodding at me as I talk that I realize I'm mansplaining to her. I mean, of course she wants to listen to me explain what's on the page, she only wrote it.

It's always refreshing when someone in this industry gives you a direct answer in good time. Whether it's in film or TV, on stage or in a classroom the fact that a person responds clearly to an offer isn't just respectful, it places power and status back into the hands of the person who made the offer. In my experience, only the best artistic directors, producers, directors and literary departments at theatres do this.

Thursday 4 April

Lolita   I am in South Africa at Thula Thula Game Reserve in KwaZulu-Natal. I am here researching *The Elephant Whisperer*, a stage adaptation I will write in September based on the book by Lawrence Anthony who used to run Thula Thula. We are here as a family, taking a holiday at the same time.

Adrian and I are in a suite and the girls have their own chalet. We are fed gourmet meals three times a day and have two game drives a day – one at 6.30 am and one at 4.00 pm. We travel around the reserve and see elephants, rhino, giraffe, zebra, nyala, buffalo, impala and more.

There are twenty-nine elephants here and I have seen many of the ones written about in the book. They are towering, majestic and curious. They come right up to the jeep and look at us whilst we look at them. I have heard the rumbling sound through which they communicate. This is a trip of a lifetime.

The girls are loving it. Even though a baby spitting cobra slithered into their room the other day and Lila, who knows a lot about animals and reptiles, identified it, called us on her mobile whilst keeping her younger sister safely away from it. We sprinted over to their cabin and alerted the staff, who got rid of it.

It's very luxurious here but very real.

We are staying here for four nights and then we will move on. The sights, sounds, smells, feel of this place, as well as the chats I've had with various members of Lawrence's family, have really informed the story I will write. I find it invaluable to visit places you are about to create on stage; it helps add detail that can only come from experience.

Monday 8 April

Adrian   The Thula Thula reserve is fantastic and we are all having a good time here. I am trying to sing a little every day to get my voice ready for *Sweet Charity* rehearsals when I get back to London. Even though we are on holiday, I can see Lolita working. She interviews members of Lawrence's family as well as talking to the Thula Thula staff members, most of whom are black. She wants the Zulu perspective on the story of the reserve and the presence of the elephants.

Lolita   We are in St Lucia on the eastern coast of South Africa, on the outskirts of iSimangaliso Wetland Park. Yesterday we saw hippos and crocodiles on a boat trip on the estuary.

Today we are on a half-day safari and snorkelling trip. We drove through the park and saw warthogs, kudu, antelope, zebra, white rhino, buffalo, vervet monkeys, gnu and had a very close encounter with a black rhino. We sit watching it for ages as it works out whether to charge us or not. It doesn't.

This trip is amazing. It is bringing to life elements of *The Elephant Whisperer* and parts of story that don't yet exist. I am also reading a book about the Truth and Reconciliation Commission in South Africa in 1996, which is giving me an insight into the truth underpinning this beautiful country.

It is an enlightening trip. Feel very privileged to be here.

Wednesday 17 April

Lolita   I am typing 'rehearsal draft' onto this script of *Pi*. I have been writing this for almost two years. I saw director Max on Monday to get his notes on the workshop draft. They are detailed and minimal – hurrah! I am so used to reams and reams of notes that I feel a little giddy with how few of them there are. I also still feel like I am in South Africa with elephants as I listen to the notes on *Pi*. This is an intense time.

Anyway, I am writing 'rehearsal draft' on the title page. I address my email to producer Simon, producer Rob at Sheffield Crucible Theatre, Max and agent Katie. I press 'send'.

Nothing more I can do till we start rehearsals in May.

Adrian   After a few afternoons' rehearsal and one preview, it's the press night for *Sweet Charity* at the Donmar Warehouse.

Lots of nerves. I'm slightly under rehearsed. I haven't gotten to know the cast that well. I haven't spent as much time with them as I would have if I had been through the full rehearsal process.

It is a lot of fun playing a role like this. I dance on, jive my way through the song with the wonderful company, have a blast and run off after high note. I think I'm on stage for a total of three minutes.

Once I'm back in the dressing room, I tuck myself into a corner by a window and work away at a new draft of *Lottery Boy*. It has taken me a long time to get this new draft out and I'm determined to finish it while I do the show here.

Friday 19 April

Lolita   I am sitting in the garden of a pub in Highbury and Islington with director Leo getting his thoughts on the last draft of *Invisible Cities*. His notes are more questions – elements that he feels are missing or unanswered. We talk around it and I think we reach some good conclusions and ideas. They are fine-tuning ideas rather than structural change. Thank goodness. I tell him I will write this up in a week after I have finished my draft of *Politically Correct*, which I know the producers are getting very restless for. He is fine with that timing. It would give the actors and creatives three weeks to study before we start.

I returned from South Africa exactly a week ago. I remember feeling tense as soon as we got home because I had so much work to do. I am relieved and very pleased that I am delivering things in time. My next deadline is to hand in *Politically Correct* next week.

The sun is shining and hot today. Lovely.

Tuesday 23 April

Lolita   I am at The Globe having a coffee with producer Malu from the Roundhouse. We are slowly advancing on *Testaments*. I have been in touch with John McGrath, artistic director of MIF, to see if this might interest him for MIF 2021. MIF's remit is to take artistic risks and push the envelope of artistry. John likes the idea and is putting it on their long list for consideration.

It is a good meeting with Malu. We work out when we need to approach various creatives and how to advance. This will be a big project of five independent monologues.

I will write one of them about a homeless man in his sixties who tells us how he came to live on the streets – the tragedies he experienced, who he was before and how it brought him some peace to give up what was left of his life. We meet him when he's layered in clothing, using plastic bags to keep warm and as he travels, he loses layers until by the end, ready for his interment, he is returned to who he really was.

Later in the day I attend my first meeting as a trustee for the Royal Victoria Hall Foundation. My job has been to assess two applications by theatre companies asking for funding and write a report. Today the nine trustees and secretary of the company discuss all the applications. It is a very pleasant afternoon and a strong reminder of the passion and hard work that lies in making all theatre.

It is the evening and I am meeting my friend Romola for the press night of *All My Sons* at the Old Vic. I worked with Romola a few years back and we really got on. It is nice to catch up with her. The play is classic and traditionally done, with Sally Field and Bill Pullman starring. I am a huge Sally Field fan and she doesn't disappoint. I enjoyed it but I realise how muscular theatre is now and with the diversification of the voices we are hearing and allowing through, this feels less vibrant, less current.

Thursday 25 April

Adrian   Before a performance of *Sweet Charity*, I have a meeting with Anne Mensah at the Hospital Club. Anne was the executive producer of the first series of *Curfew* and *Riviera*, when she ran Sky's drama department. She's great to work for and has a keen eye for a good story.

I had sent her two ideas I've been working on for a couple of long-running TV series. Her feedback is positive and quick. She likes them both and immediately gives me a few notes that I can see make the stories better and gives them a greater arc.

She is now working for Netflix UK and wants to keep an eye on the ideas as I develop them.

Tuesday 7 May

Lolita   I am on a long call to Kate Prince about her ideas for *Message in a Bottle* – the dance show based around Sting and The Police's music. This is Kate's idea and is for Sadler's Wells and I am dramaturging for her. We spend over two hours talking through her ideas and storyline aiming for each song she has chosen to earn its place in this story. I love Kate's work. Her company ZooNation made me see the brilliance of hip hop and street dance in a classical form. She has a great way of telling urban stories with heart and humour, so I am very pleased to be working with her.

The ideas are strong, but she just needs a sounding board to find her story and help with ordering it. As writer, choreographer and creator of this work she is simultaneously thinking of the particular dancers she has cast, the shifts of the set and the numbers of dancers available after each dance, as well as telling a story. It's dense work but enjoyable, particularly as I am coming up with alternative ideas and then have no responsibility to write them.

Wednesday 8 May

Lolita   I am in east London with our personal manager and publicist Tina Price doing a photo shoot for *Good Housekeeping* magazine. I always enjoy things like this because people choose clothes and looks for you that you would never think of yourself.

The stylist puts me in bold and bright, very fitted outfits. A pink two-piece suit, a leopard-print dress and an orange/red jumpsuit with heels I can't walk in but which look great. The make-up is glam and I am wearing false eyelashes for the first time in my life. Tina always makes sure everything runs smoothly and that you feel comfortable. I do. It's great fun.

Thursday 16 May

Lolita   I am in Patisserie Valerie near Goodge Street with Adrian meeting Sean Foley, new artistic director of Birmingham Rep, and his deputy, Amit Sharma. I was in *Hamlet* directed by Ken Branagh at RADA with Sean in 2017 and we both had plays on in Ken Branagh's season at the Garrick in 2016. This is about my new play, *Calmer*. He offers us (Adrian is going to direct it) a slot in his inaugural season in Autumn 2020. It is brilliant news. He suggests the 300-seat studio, which would work brilliantly, but if we manage to get strong casting he will consider main house. It is very exciting.

I wrote this play in 2014. It discusses motherhood and chaos, how we give conflicting messages to our daughters no matter what age. It's called *Calmer* because it's about panic and passing that on to our kids. I will also act in it, which is something Sean understands because he is an actor, director and writer.

Sunday 19 May

Adrian   I am at a RADA reunion. I left thirty years ago and can't believe it's been that long. As we were all milling about in the bar; my reaction to people was, of course, based on how I knew them. Memories start flooding in and the first part of any conversation is taken up with the facts of the past that you may have forgotten. 'Do you remember so and so . . .', 'oh man, that day when we all used to . . .', etc. Then you ask how they are and as they explain their lives – what has passed, good and bad – I find myself staring at a face in which thirty years of life fast-forwards in front of me, summarized in five minutes of conversation. That teenager that I trained with thirty years ago is now wearing someone older.

Monday 20 May

Lolita   I am in the rehearsal room for the first day of *Pi*. We have thirteen actors, many creatives, several producers and production staff. There are over thirty people in the room. Tim shows us the designs and they look great. Then Andrew plays us some of the music he's composed – beautiful. Then we read the script.

It is so good to hear the script with all the different voices. It actually reads very well and there are lots of laughs and lightness in it. Unusually for me at a read-through, I can hear that it is pretty tight: the structure works and the voices are defined. I have been writing this so intensely for the last two years and constantly solving problems, answering people's questions, trying to make sense of what Yann and I are trying to say, that to hear it all playing fairly well is amazing.

We are told that the show will run for three weeks at Sheffield. I know it's just a first outing, but it seems a hell of a lot of work for three weeks. Anyway, I guess we will iron out problems in this room that will hold us in good stead in others. It suddenly occurred to me that we will do this work for Sheffield and then hopefully have to do it all over again.

We had a bit of an issue with the rehearsal room, which is very small considering we have a prototype boat and thirteen actors. We are not able to mark the stage out on the floor – it's too small. We all make calls to producers and try to see if we can change rooms at some point. We'll see how that goes; it's a question of money.

In the afternoon, Finn does some general puppetry work with the company. It's great to hear him talking about how to focus on the puppet and fill it with purpose, intent and meaning. The actors learn fast, whilst some of them are very experienced already.

Then we all sit round in a circle and chat about the themes of the play. It's reassuring to hear people pick up on so many of the elements I have laid underneath the text. And also to hear that the story works on several levels, which I have aimed to make clear *and* hidden. The questions and discussion it provokes are very pleasing.

Thursday 23 May

Adrian I head over to WAK Studios to have my first session on 'I Wish' for Children In Need, with my producer Jonathan Quarmby.

Shaun and Polly Dooley have had things move pretty quickly since our earlier conversations about this album. I had an informal meet-up for a photo with some of the other artists during which I mentioned why I chose the song. I began to explain how the bass line and vocals might sound on the album, trying to let the producers hear what I meant by making sounds with my mouth. Then someone pipes up 'You should do it a cappella'. I laugh until I catch Mark De-Lisser's eye. Mark is nodding seriously at me. He's our vocal coach and thinks I should give it a try. I'm a little nervous about tackling one of Stevie's most famous songs a cappella and have tried to get my voice ready over the previous few days.

I'm unprepared for the camera team that are waiting for me on arrival. I know they need to record and capture each bit of the work, but to some extent their presence makes me wary of experimenting and getting things wrong. After a few hours we have managed to lay down the drums, the bass, the lead vocals and a section of the harmonies.

I think it sounds ok, but I could so easily make a well-meaning fool of myself here. I know it's for a great cause but I'm quite worried as I leave.

Tuesday 28 May

Lolita   I am in the first day of rehearsals for *Invisible Cities* at Rambert on the South Bank. The morning is spent reading the new draft, which works well – mostly.

Director Leo gives a two-hour presentation to the whole team. I am a little taken aback because there are over seventy people in the room: all the dancers, cast, creatives, crew, producers and teams from MIF, Rambert, 59 Productions and Sadler's Wells. It's a big crowd.

Leo talks through the ideas and designs and inspirations for the whole production. It is, of course, based entirely on the script I have written – that's daunting. There has been so much work before and during my writing, so much coordination of different elements and disciplines. It is interesting to see the whole concept explained; much of it I know, but some of it is new.

At the end, Leo gets everyone to introduce themselves. There is something so simple but essential about giving your name and profession. Instantly we are a team working together and no longer strangers.

In the afternoon, we work with the actors on the script. There are many questions, some of which I can answer and others which we discuss and emerge at a solution. I can often taste what I want but need to solve the problem on my own. People are generally very respectful of that. We do good work and work through two of the seven scenes – it's a lot to take on.

As I head home, Max calls as promised with an update of events in today's *Pi* rehearsal room. It was a good day, he says, with a few minor script changes requested, which I will deal with tomorrow when I am with them in the room. There is one slightly bigger script change but to be honest, they all feel relatively minor now because the main structure is sorted.

I feel like I am responsible for everyone because my words have to make sense for them to do it. I don't know if I take it all too much to heart but I write as an actress, with feeling; that's how this works for me.

I get an email from my acting agent for an audition on Friday! It always happens this way. When things are very full on, more piles on top. But it is a great audition so I need to make this work. It's a good part in a period drama for Netflix. I must rise to the occasion, no question.

In the evening, I went for dinner with Adrian and his brother Scott, who has been staying with us for some time while he works in London. It was nice to have an adult moment.

Wednesday 29 May

Adrian　A few months ago, Sharon White had written to me asking me to join an advisory panel at Ofcom to feed back on some of the ideas that the team there felt could rebalance the lack of diversity on our screens. Today is our first meeting.

Trying to make these changes to our industry is a painfully slow process. So much red tape slows progress down as many people hold to an idea that positive racial discrimination is against the law because it is still racial discrimination. It is also difficult to report on figures to see how the industry is doing if the questionnaires are only being filled in on a voluntary basis. If this remains the case, then there is no compelling reason for many independent production companies to comply.

Friday 31 May

Lolita　It's been a tough week, not in terms of the work but in terms of me being able to focus on these two stories simultaneously.

Wednesday was the most challenging. The morning with *Invisible Cities*, the afternoon with *Pi*. Many questions needing answers in both rooms. I think I did it. Don't know if I did it well, but I did it.

I am in the *Invisible Cities* room today at the end of the first week. Today is the first time I see the actors and dancers working together. Choreographer Sidi Larbi Cherkaoui is here today so the whole creative team is present.

In terms of canvases, these shows are big. When I was watching the actors in *Pi* yesterday, I saw they are working so hard and the story leaves no prisoners. It plunged on, getting more and more intense. And the scale of *Invisible Cities* is hard to imagine because all three disciplines of words, dance and projection are being used to their limit. None of them is in relief to the others.

Anyway, I am glad that it is the end of this week. It's been about stamina, clarity and staying open to all the many voices who need the story to be clearer or better.

Saturday 1 June

Lolita   It is my birthday today and I am fifty. When I look at that number, it feels weighty and experienced, but when I think of myself I feel like I'm just getting going.

I had a lovely day with the family.

On Monday I have to deliver the new drafts of both plays – all the changes that we've worked on in rehearsals and a few that I've been left to mull over. I have come home every evening and written one or the other. After Monday, the rehearsals will become a different thing for me – more intense. Less about the smaller moments and more about the arc of both pieces.

Anyway, today I did not work. I have been with Adrian and the girls. I have arrived in a new decade and who knows what it will bring.

Thursday 6 June

Lolita   I am in Sheffield in the rehearsal room for *Pi*. I arrived on Tuesday morning and go home tonight because I have *Invisible Cities* rehearsal in London tomorrow.

I have the story elements for *Pi*, but as the actors and Max and Finn work through it, it becomes clear that the story needs focusing or shifting.

Yesterday I finished a new script for the cast with all the changes, and there are many that have been coming up. And then today Max pointed out that the first half still isn't working and the story needs restructuring again.

Of course, what that means is that you have to shift the progression of internal elements of the play and reshape the joins between the scenes. My heart sank. No lie. Especially when you are in the room with the actors. There is nowhere to hide.

I think what I find more exhausting is the much-needed questioning of the scripts by so many people. In *Pi*, there are thirteen actors and six creatives. In *Invisible Cities*, there are two actors and maybe ten creatives. And I have to answer or solve the problem then and there.

So now I am on the train in the evening, heading back to London after a long day of working through many of the text-based scenes and I am restructuring the first half and retightening the second half so that Max can move forward. Because of my acting I am very aware that when the words don't work, you get stuck. So the sooner I can unlock the words for the actors and the true order of the story for everyone else, the sooner they can do their best work.

Friday 7 June

Lolita   End of the week. I am at Rambert in the rehearsal room after three days. They have been working on without me and I have tried to stay in the loop from Sheffield with script changes and rewrites but it has been difficult. Jules, the stage manager, and Rebecca, the assistant director, have been in regular contact but some things got lost. And then of course in some sections the two actors know something doesn't work but are unable to solve it because they are restricted by what I've written.

So I came in and listened and rewrote the opening speech for Danny, who is playing Kublai Khan, and rewrote a section later in the play where Leo wanted to add a big section from the book.

I am getting much better at asking for what the director/actor needs and interpreting it into emotional action. I feel totally unfit physically because I sit on my butt all day. But I feel intellectually *very* fit and like I'm moving faster than ever.

By the end of the day, I had a new draft ready for them all to work from. There have been so many changes and the dance elements and projection ideas keep changing – so I have incorporated them into the narrative, which will enable the actors to be free and play.

Friday. Hurray. I have to wonder around town, have dinner and wait till 9.15 pm to pick up my youngest from the theatre with her friend. The other side of things.

Saturday 8 June

Adrian Went along to see the Pushkin Drama Theatre production of *The Knight of the Burning Pestle*, directed by Declan Donnellan.

It was their final performance and afterwards Declan and Nick invited me along to join them and the company for a few drinks at their flat. It was good to see them. We sat in the garden talking for what seemed like hours. Declan spoke with me about a new book he is writing. As we caught up he mentioned an interest in physics. I think I might have gone into full geek mode as we found an appreciation for acting, direction and energy that adhered to the same rules as other bodies in space. Bodies that, big or small, would change based upon their relationship to one another. People are arguably the most complex biological forms on the planet, but in relationships we obey the same rules as atoms.

Everything becomes relative. A person can only be described as cruel or kind in comparison to the world around them. A point can only be hot or cold based on how we see the area around that point. The question of whether we behave in the ways that we do because of nature or nurture are most interesting for the actor if we believe that our behaviour is based on nurture.

It's much more interesting to explore a person in this way because what influences us is relative to how we feel about it. The influences are not fixed; they keep shifting.

What creates a person, in any given moment, is past history and present obstacle. If, on the other hand, a character is built because of their nature, we then enter territory that is very boring for the actor and also boring in performance. A character of nature is thus, says thus and does thus just because they do. Response to external stimuli is very limited. They are fixed and to some degree won't change because their condition is not relatable to their present circumstance.

All of the characters that are noteworthy in Shakespeare's canon are based on the nurture principle. The soliloquies are full of the psychological changes that map out a person surprising themselves with their response to external stimuli. So much so, that they need to make the audience a touchstone as they try to map out their thoughts and gain some perspective. Animals are built on nature, while humans use their intellect and relationships to chart a path that is different. Humans are built as they respond.

Yeah, like I said . . . full geek mode.

Wednesday 12 June

Adrian   The Children in Need team have got me a rehearsal with MC Zani, for a beatbox session. He is an incredibly skilled beatboxer and has listened to 'I Wish' in order to pull out some of the sounds I will need to make in order to make the song work. During the session, I gently coax him to show us a bit of what he can do . . . The camera is on him and he lets fly. It's pretty amazing stuff. He starts to show me how he makes all the sounds and I see what an art it is. I think I may have bitten off more than I can chew here.

Lolita   I am in the rehearsal room for *Pi*. The cast and team are working incredibly hard. They did a run of the first half yesterday when I arrived – this show is epic. So much happens and it all requires precision, detail, performance and energy. The structure wasn't right. So Max, associate director Hannah and I sat at lunch trying to work out what was best.

I find these moments difficult. Where there is something fundamental to be solved and it is up to me. My brain feels pretty fried at the minute, so clarity isn't there. But I make myself remember that often, when you're acting, you do your best work when you're tired because you respond instinctively rather than with intellect. Maybe that is true of writing. The answers come from somewhere else.

It felt a little overwhelming that the structure wasn't right. But as we talked it out, it became clear that the issue is the first half of the first half and the solutions are there. Max always presents clear thinking and Hannah brought my attention to the detail that was already there. It was much appreciated.

I left rehearsals early and went to do the work in my hotel room. I always feel better when I start to do them, otherwise they sit in the forefront of my brain without being sorted. It was fine. Max said we need to cut five or six pages and that happened. Tighter, leaner, better.

I have my audition on Friday for that nice TV job. It's a high-status part in a quality TV series on Netflix. Would love to get it. Have to push myself and try.

Thursday 13 June

Adrian   I'm happy that I've managed to be present for this year's Lilian Baylis Awards. It normally takes place on the Old Vic stage but as the theatre is being refurbished, we are in the rehearsal room at the top of the building.

I've seen old black-and-white photos of the National Theatre company rehearsing in that room. Gielgud and Olivier among many others standing around, working a scene from something or other, and here we are today to hand out various financial awards to students in their second year at drama school.

I was one of the first recipients of the award when it started in 1986 and as Valerie Colgan introduces me to speak, she reminds everyone of this fact. Valerie goes on to give a breakdown of my career that is very flattering but also incredibly detailed: she includes dates of performances, quotes from reviews, certain bits of information about the rehearsals and the venues I've performed in as well as the screen-work I've done. By the time I step up to speak, I don't know what to say.

After the ceremony I have a chat with the students, including one who has recently played *Othello* at his drama school. I can see the process of playing the character has unsettled him a little. As we leave the theatre and talk, I find myself being quite honest about the way it unsettled me too, in performance. I don't want him feeling that the negative effects of the character have only been felt by him.

Whenever I meet actors who have played *Othello*, telling me they had a fantastic time, that it was all great fun and that they really enjoyed it . . . part of me believes they haven't done it right.

Saturday 15 June

Adrian   On a flight to LA now to attend the premiere of *The Rook*. Starz seems to really believe in the show. Their marketing team is working really hard to get it into the publics sphere of attention.

It's a 'blue-carpet' ceremony, as that's the main colour used in the show's marketing, at the Getty Museum, followed by an outdoor party with themed cocktails and a DJ.

It's great to see the cast again as we walk the carpet, do the interviews and sell the show.

It's a very short trip. I will get home in time for Lolita to travel to Sheffield and Manchester as *Invisible Cities* and *Life of Pi* go through their final stages of rehearsal before opening.

Friday 21 June

Adrian   Another session with Jonathan Quarmby on the Stevie Wonder track. After my session with him, my voice is really tired. I've been hitting my highest notes in order to make the sounds of the trumpets and the backing vocals, as well as blasting out the lead vocal line again and again.

Afterwards I head over to the Soho Hotel to record an interview for The Sky Arts Awards, as the recipient of the special award this year is Sir Lenny Henry.

Lolita   I returned from Sheffield last night. It was another full-on frantic trip on *Pi*. We had a run on Wednesday with a lot of different people watching. Mostly the narrative worked but two major scenes didn't. So I stayed up late, got up early, didn't sleep well and wrote.

My head is full and sleep is not guaranteed. But having children has taught me that you can function without sleep; you just have to embrace it and not fight. Funny what you learn along life's way.

I had to cut some of the play and give those cuts to the cast. I explained the cuts to the cast. Often a lack of communication is the problem in these situations. They were very gracious and took them. I know that everyone needs stability as they gear up to tech and being in the theatre, so I felt bad for not being able to provide that. I tried to remind myself that I am supplying narrative and that is what I must stay focused on.

Had a wobble, feeling unable to deliver, feeling tired and on my own in the task ahead. Spoke to Adrian and felt better.

So today I am back in London and it is the last day at Rambert. But first I am picked up in a cab and taken to BBC Broadcasting House, where I meet Tina to record *Loose Ends* for Radio 4. I am interviewed by Sara Cox, who is lovely and asks interesting questions. She asked me about my drama teacher, Miss Stack, and it was so nice to talk about her and her influence.

Then Tina and I went back to Rambert where I had my picture taken for the forthcoming *Financial Times* profile piece. Afterwards I have a quiet lunch on my own on the South Bank, where my brain feels like it's still moving whilst I am still.

Later I go into rehearsals for the last time to see a run of *Invisible Cities*. It has come on hugely. They have done so much work on it. I had notes on the narrative but Leo is so busy he's hard to pin down, so I emailed them to him as requested. I don't know if they'll be implemented or acted upon.

I spend the evening putting all changes from the two scripts into final versions. And then I email both new drafts to the long line of people in each show who need them tomorrow. By the end of this evening it is done. Five intense, demanding and exhausting weeks and I have not slackened off or left any question unresolved. I did my best.

The next stage of previews is about to begin but as for rewriting – that is over.

Wednesday 26 June

Lolita   I am on the train heading up to Manchester for the final leg of this mammoth journey. In two weeks' time, both shows will be up and my job done and they will be off my plate. I've had a couple of days in London. I wasn't sleeping so well while I was away and it's very nice to catch up on home comforts. I am feeling a little recharged.

It was announced today that *Invisible Cities* is going to Brisbane Festival in September. So that's good. On it goes.

I am at Euston waiting for my train to Manchester. The first two are cancelled! That's a great start. The next train looks like it will be crammed and everyone races with their wheelie cases determined to get a seat. I decide to take it easy and look after myself, I go for a later train and easily get a seat without the anxiety of everyone who is late and cross.

I get to Manchester where I am met by John, the artist liaison, and taken to the Dakota Hotel to check in before heading straight over to Mayfield. I have been talking about it for so long, I didn't realize it was right next to Piccadilly Station. Of course. It's a disused train depot. When we get there, I see what a mammoth task it has been. There are Portakabins for every department and the stage is looking fantastic. Jenny Melville, the designer, has done a great job and it is wonderful to see her drawings in reality.

The tech is epic. They are behind. There are so many elements to factor in and of course the space is much bigger than the rehearsal rooms at Rambert. I say hello to people, sit in the dark and watch. Leo has a few line requests, which I go and do in the green room area where there is daylight. Otherwise I don't envy this tech. It looks hard. I say hi to the actors – they seem okay.

This is the stage where you're trying to hold on to your performance and the narrative. The digital has not been introduced until now and it feels like a character hasn't made its entrance at all in rehearsals. So suddenly they will have to play with a whole new element. That's hard.

I leave the tech after the afternoon. I have a pain in my hip. It's muscular, I think, but I have been so sedentary being a writer – sitting in one place or another – that my body is starting to object. It's painful.

I get to the hotel and eat and relax for a moment and then head to the Royal Exchange Theatre where I had my second job in 1991. It's great to come back. It is much more compact than I remember. I am seeing *Hobson's Choice*, adapted by Tanika Gupta and designed by Rosa. It's great. Charming, a fine story, wittily told. After the epic unfolding of *Invisible Cities*, where the narrative is sometimes at odds with the other elements, it's great to see a straightforward good story.

I have been thinking of the rewrite I need to do for *Politically Correct*. With all the weird things happening in western politics, the version I have written is actually happening in real life. I need to rethink it and work out why I'm telling it. I need to make it about a more extreme situation that's about to get worse.

Thursday 27 June

Adrian   It's the Children in Need album recording day at Abbey Road Studios. Jasmine is with me. She has a fantastic voice and enjoys music so much I wanted her to see how it all gets put together for an album.

Jim Broadbent, Suranne Jones, Himesh Patel, Shaun Dooley, Olivia Colman and Helena Bonham Carter are all there on the day as we are going to record the lead single together, Labi Siffre's 'It Must Be Love'. I have the first line in the song and need to float it quite high across the break in my voice. Really not a good thing to try without a full and proper warm-up. We stand in a semicircle at microphones, everyone watching and listening. The music starts, our vocal coach Mark De-Lisser conducts us all and then counts me in to sing the sweet high notes that will begin the song. I take a breath, open my mouth and produce a sound like a strangled chicken.

I sound terrible on the next few attempts too.

It's quite a buzz being in those studios recording songs in this way. I think I liked it a little too much. Singing 'I Wish' in a booth while receiving critique from the producers and the engineer in the control room was a great experience. Hope I get the chance to do it again.

I get home and watch David Harewood's documentary *Psychosis and Me*. I know Dave as we were at drama school at the same time. I remember hearing vaguely about his troubles after he had left training but seeing the details, as he recounts his state of mind at the time, I find incredibly moving. The pain and fear he recounts is visceral and upsetting. A very brave and honest programme.

Lolita   I am on the train to Sheffield. I check in to my hotel then head straight over to the Crucible Theatre. The company of *Pi* have been in tech all week. It's nice to see everyone. Max runs a very good, calm, clear tech. There's a lot to do and the team are working incredibly hard but it looks brilliant.

The cast are still good-humoured – always a challenge at tech. I can see everyone is tired. The work isn't completely finished but we have an open dress rehearsal tonight – a Crucible tradition – where they give very low-priced tickets to whoever wants to come.

There are a few hundred people here. It's the first time the cast and team have run the show all together. Everyone is nervous. I am intrigued to see what this is – you need the audience to gauge it. Where do they collectively laugh? Where do they gasp and where are they attentively silent? It's a really good barometer of how the whole machine is working.

The cast and team do so well; the story is achieved and told and most elements happen. Some of it is breathtakingly magical and some of it is so devastating. The beginning of each act needs attention.

There is collective relief and disbelief that they all got through it and the Crucible buy us all a drink afterwards.

I haven't seen anything like this before. *Pi* has a strange mix of childlike storytelling, visceral truth, difficult and ugly choices and pain. I think it works but maybe it's *too* interesting, maybe we need genres so we don't stretch too far and make new choices. I don't know. Let's see how this goes.

Max says we need to cut five minutes of the second half. He's not been too keen on the magic island from the start. I've kept hold of it because I think it's iconic in the book and fun and dark but maybe I'll have to let it go. There are difficult choices at every turn, but all for the good of the story.

Saturday 29 June

Lolita I meet with Jack Bradley, who is dramaturg on *Pi*, and Max this morning. We have a long session discussing two scenes that aren't working completely. The zoo scene, which is the second scene of the play, has become unclear because in trying to introduce so many elements of this production the story has got diluted and lost. It is too early in the show to lose story.

Yesterday I was very down because all problems were brought to me, as if they were script issues. But today I see that they are everyone's problems and I am being asked to solve them with writing.

The pressure has been incredible. All these people are working so hard and then when things don't work I feel responsible for it. The preview last night went really well. We had a standing ovation again and the actors really upped their game, so today I felt buoyed up.

After notes, I go to write all afternoon in my hotel – reshaping the narrative of the zoo scene, introducing a joke in the market scene to allow the audience to feel they can laugh at the religious leaders on stage. And we have made the bold choice of cutting the magic island scene. I have fought for this scene from the start. I like it but the consensus has been against it and its not working at the minute. I can see the script for this section is not yet right but also the design is not working and the actors are struggling. It is at the end of the play so needs to be wonderful and it's not. Tonight we will cut it and see what that does. I rewrite the join to make it work for tonight.

The show is tricky. The revolve brakes down. The actors are really tired. An incident with a member of the audience who has dementia delays the second half. The show stops midway. It is bumpy, to say the least. I miss the island. The other creatives don't because they are unsure of how to realize it. But I will rewrite tonight and we'll see. We still get a standing ovation.

Drinks after. Everyone is knackered but battling on because ultimately I think this show says something to us all and matters.

Monday 1 July

Adrian   I'm at a read-through in Manchester for *Life*, a BBC drama written by Mike Bartlett, who I last worked with on *Trauma*.

The exec producers came along to Hampstead to see *Cost of Living* a few months ago. When I came out to meet them afterwards, this project was mentioned in conversation. I know I wouldn't have got this job if I hadn't done the play at Hampstead and thankfully timings have been worked out with the possible second series of *The Rook*.

The cast at the read-through are people I've admired for years. Elaine Paige is among them. Strange, as I've been watching her online while trying to learn the lyrics and harmonies for 'I Know Him So Well'. I don't think I'll mention it. I might come across as a bit of a stalker. I've been listening to the song because Jason Manford and I are going to sing a rendition for a charity event that we have coming up.

Though I'm in Manchester, Lolita is in Sheffield today working on *Pi*. She's back in Manchester in two days, so we've just missed each other.

Lolita   I am in interviews this morning. I speak to a journalist from A Younger Theatre about *Pi*. She was very nice and we chatted about process and challenges. Then I spoke to someone for BBC Look North about much the same. They are filming some of the show and interviewing us all for TV tomorrow.

I am now in the theatre with the company and Max. I have spent the last couple of days rewriting some of the scenes. We tech the new zoo scene. It has been difficult to know what the show needs at certain moments but between us we work it out. The puppets and design and style of the show needs its own introduction so all the characters I have created need to be introduced at the same time. The zoo has been very important and not working. So after redraft after redraft I think we're almost there.

The company are doing so well. They are obviously tired, there have been couple of injuries because the work is so demanding, but they soldier on and absorb the script changes. We tech through the new configuration for the zoo, which Finn has made clearer in movement. I have written a clearer story, the design, sound, lights, digital are working much better together and Max is holding the whole thing. The cast have a few queries with the script but it's great to have a library of lines from which we can all now draw.

I sneak off in the afternoon for a massage – a gift from my fantastic agent Katie – because I was feeling the strain. It is an absolute tonic and a reminder that there is life outside of these two projects.

The third preview goes well. The show is better, tighter. The audience are on their feet again at the end. The zoo works much better. The acting gets a little saggy at the end so it doesn't quite punch as it should, but they are on their feet. It's a detail.

Producer Simon Friend is in tonight for the first time. He is very pleased. From that first chat we had that this needs to be somewhere between *Lion King* and *War Horse*, and now here we are and it is. I can't quite believe it is almost done.

I go back to my hotel and send Max my notes and thoughts on tonight. I am in Manchester tomorrow so won't be around when they tech and work the new opening to the market scene.

I get an email from the Rambert company manager about *Invisible Cities*. They were meant to dress tonight but were behind and so didn't. They have their first preview tomorrow, which will run without a full tech run before. The tensions and nerves must be high. I will see when I get there.

Tuesday 2 July

Adrian　Jason Manford has very kindly come down to London to be a special guest at the Primary Shakespeare Company (PSC) gala. The PSC organization is run by Neil Carter and Luke Hollowell-Williams and over the past ten years has been getting Shakespeare and performance back on the curriculum at inner-city schools in London. Each play is used as a foundation for the work the kids do that year in English, creative writing, maths and science, using the stories of Shakespeare to teach the kids essential life skills including team-building and creative thinking. It's a great charity and I'm proud to be a patron alongside Billie Piper and Hugh Bonneville, who is compering this evenings proceedings.

Jason and I had a great time on *Guys and Dolls*, but never got the chance to sing together. Tonight we are going to remedy that. We're going to sing 'I Know Him So Well' as a love duet to the highest bidder in the audience.

Jason gets on stage and does a very funny twenty minutes of material. We are all chuckling away when he announces that we're going to sing a song. I get up on stage and we start the bidding. The highest bidder, called Mark, makes his way onto stage and as the music starts he stands between Jason and me. We both have the lyrics in our hands so that we know who is going to sing which line at each particular moment.

Mark knows 'I Know Him So Well' and likes it, so decides he wants to join in and make it fun. He takes my lyrics away from me in order to sing along. I now can't see what I'm singing so decide to keep going from memory.

As Jason begins his second verse, Mark kneels down in front of him . . . we are all very close and people are filming this on their phones. Suddenly the idea of 'knowing' someone takes on a Biblical meaning. The audience are giggling. Jason and I manage to finish the song,

Even though I may have ended my career with a three-man romp on stage to the tune of 'I Know Him So Well', the evening is a great success for PSC. They manage to raise £70,000, which will help them carry on their work for a few more years.

Lolita　I leave my giant suitcase at the hotel in Sheffield and travel to Manchester this morning. I check in to my hotel here and go straight to

Mayfield. The space has changed, become more finished, safer for visitors. They haven't managed to do a dress run and the first preview is tonight. They spend the afternoon running sections of the show. It is so ambitious and vast with so many elements. They get through it and then it is dinner break.

I am back at my hotel to put my feet up. I feel slightly disoriented. When I'm in the lift going up to my room, I get confused. Which floor is it? Which city is it? I have an hour in my room and then go back to Mayfield for the first preview.

There is a big audience here – maybe 500 or 600 people. It begins.

They all do really well. Pushing through the scenes. The scene changes are problematic – enormous pieces of scenery that need an effortless turnaround. It adds loads of time onto the show. The use of water in the show is unpredictable and the dancers slip on it a little. They push through.

The video projection is not what I thought it would be and so it takes me a while to adjust. The story I wrote is there but interrupted by video, as opposed to aided by it.

The show was meant to be about ninety minutes straight through, but because of logistical issues with a huge team of stage management, we have an interval and it runs at two hours and forty minutes.

I go back to my hotel at the end and try to think of possible helpful solutions. I cut the script and try to suggest a narrative through the video projection that will help the story. It's a bit late to impose narrative, I know – but always worth a go.

I am sure they will work like crazy to tighten and reduce the piece.

Wednesday 3 July

Lolita I do some notes on *Invisible Cities* and email them. I go to the station and travel back to Sheffield.

My hotel isn't ready until 3.00 pm, so I stop in the Writers' Room at the Lyric and try to work on *Politically Correct*.

I head back to the hotel and have my giant suitcase again. I work out my outfits for tonight's opening here, being on TV on Friday and opening night Friday evening. I sort through my jewellery, my shoes and pack accordingly.

In the evening, I head over to the Crucible for the regional opening night of *Life of Pi*. It's odd not having Adrian here. This is a big deal and I'm on my own. But it means I am very present.

The theatre is full. I watch the show. By the interval people gasp, caught up in the story, and by the end they are on their feet cheering before the actors are on stage. I feel very proud.

The last time I was in this kind of situation was when *Red Velvet* opened in the West End. I am so pleased that I wrote *Life of Pi* – it has cost a lot of time and angst but this creative team are extraordinary and working with Max has been a gift. He has been a great collaborator, a strong guide, a friend and a sounding board.

I have a couple of drinks with the company, who all look lovely and bright. They work so hard and they give the show everything they have. I love actors.

Bed. Manchester tomorrow.

Friday 5 July

Lolita   I am up at 6.30 am because I am on *BBC Breakfast* in Salford talking about both projects. I am very tired and nervous. I hope I make sense. The make-up lady does wonders and the five-minute interview flies past. I feel like I gabbled because there's much to talk about, but I rang Adrian and he said I didn't. Tina is with me for the next few days. Behind the scenes she has been booking all my travel and accommodation and press. It's great to have her here.

After *BBC Breakfast*, I do an interview on BBC Manchester radio.

Then after that we go to Mayfield and I do an interview for BBC 2, as they are doing a piece on *Invisible Cities* for an arts programme.

Back to the hotel. Max needs a couple of small rewrites. Both companies need the latest script. I do that as quickly a possible then Tina and I go out for brunch.

In the afternoon, I go over to Mayfield for the actors' notes session. It's the first one I've been invited to and it is nice to put my feedback in. I leave cards and gifts for the dancers, actors and key creatives.

Back to the hotel to rest and then I meet dear friends Rhashan Stone and Olivia Williams and their beautiful daughters for tea. They have come up for opening night and to see *Pi* tomorrow. It is so nice to have good mates here. I realize what a lonely road it is to write.

I get ready for opening night. Katie Haines, my agent, is here. Annette Niemtzow, producer of *The Elephant Whisperer*, and her wife Eve have come over from NY for the opening. I meet them for the first time. Other colleagues and friends are here too. We drink champagne in the hotel bar – I am allowed this tonight. I have been very abstemious for the last few weeks in order to keep my thoughts clear and my energies up. But tonight feels like I can let go of one of these stories now.

Invisible Cities begins. The company are a little nervous and hesitant. The traffic outside is very noisy – motorbikes, sirens, trains, buses. The actors keep going. It runs smoothly. As I watch it, I can feel a great sense of relief in letting it go. No more rewriting. No more trying to find the meaning. No more working on it. It's lovely.

I see it with new eyes. The actors and the dancers are incredible. They have all upped their game and play hard. They hold the space beautifully. It is an esoteric, strange feast of enormity and scale. I don't know how you can quantify it. It has been an extraordinary thing to be a part of but I am glad it is over.

I have found new friends at Rambert which is great; I am once again a great admirer of their skill and work. They reflect the vision I have of our business – absolute quality and diversity and individual ability combined.

My group go back to the hotel for champagne and chips and bed at 2.00 am. It is done.

Saturday 6 July

Lolita   Woke up in Manchester and travelled to Sheffield with Tina. We booked into an apartment. Met friends for tea and cake. Then in the late afternoon we went to the theatre. Yann Martel, author of *Life of Pi*, is here to watch the show. Max and I did a talk with Yann for friends of the theatre. It was great, talking across our three disciplines. Very interesting to hear Yann's take on theatre versus novel writing.

Then we all went for dinner with agent Katie, producer of *The Elephant Whisperer* Annette and her wife Eve. Then we watched the show.

I haven't seen it for a couple of days so it was good to be back. The cast were tired because it is the end of the week, but their emotional life on stage was far deeper and they are more self-assured.

The auditorium was full. At the end there was a standing ovation. Yann liked it. He and his partner, Alice, seemed genuinely pleased. Great to talk about all things *Pi* with the originator of the story. We all went for drink and the cast joined us and met Yann.

It was a very good night. I was relieved and very pleased that Yann liked it. I have wanted to honour his wonderful book since I took this on and I think I did. We have his seal of approval. He has been extremely generous and trusting of me. I was very grateful for that tonight.

Monday 8 July

Adrian   Driving to Sheffield to see Lolita and attend the press night of *Life Of Pi* at the Crucible. I'm very excited to see the show, having heard every aspect of its development over the past few months.

Lolita   Had breakfast with my friend Sarah and her son who have come up to Sheffield for the opening night tonight. Spent the afternoon at the flat and had a little sleep. I am feeling jet lagged without the flying! Then Adrian and the girls arrived in the afternoon. Then we got ready for opening night and went into the theatre. I dropped off cards for everyone. I managed to find a picture of Durga on a tiger which I had printed and mounted for all the cast. It seemed apt. Then we all went to dinner before the show at 7.15 pm.

Adrian   I can feel Lolita's nerves as she sits beside us to watch the show. As the lights go down I give her hand a little squeeze. It's been a long road and she has been so calm and collaborative under pressure.

The performance is great. The direction, the acting, the puppetry, the design of set sound and lighting are all exceptional and come together seamlessly to tell the same story. The cast work themselves into a sweat as they quick change from character to animal and back again.

It is magical and moving, so much so that by the time the lights begin to dim at the end, the audience is already on its feet. I'm so proud but realize I'll have to try and keep a lid on it as I tell Lolita how great I think it is. Lila and Jasmine are beaming as they hug her and tell her what they thought.

I'm still very proud and quite excited as we head downstairs to meet the cast and creative team. I tell them how great I think the work is and feel I know each individual well but have to remind myself that I don't really know these people. I have only heard how they have felt in rehearsal and know how they overcame the technical problems they've faced because Lolita has told me in great detail. I'm probably coming across as an overexcited fan.

Lolita   The show went well. The theatre was full. The actors were a little nervous and the rhythms were a little different, but once they got into it they played it very well indeed. It felt fuller and more emotional. Hiran, who plays Pi, is really getting the arc and breadth of the character. He gives a strong performance.

A standing ovation as usual. I could get used to this!

Everyone was very effusive and kind afterwards. Adrian and the girls were beaming. Tina was so full of praise. Yann seemed delighted. Producer Simon Friend seemed pleased. All the creatives – Max, Tim, Finn, Nick, Andrew – were there and seemed pleased. It is a little overwhelming.

So now we wait for reviews and the future of this show. I feel like it will go on. It is beautiful and says so much. Time to wait to see what happens.

Wednesday 10 July

Lolita   Reviews for *Invisible Cities* are in – it gets four or three stars and is well received for its ambition. I am intrigued to read the reviews and mainly they reflect my own thoughts on the whole process – which is always reassuring.

Reviews for *Life of Pi* are amazing. Five stars and wonderful across the board. They couldn't be better. Not one dissension. I am overwhelmed. Talk of West End, touring, Broadway. Like a dream! We shall see. People are flying over from the US and travelling up to Sheffield to see it. The feedback on Twitter is amazing. So that's why it was so hard!

Adrian   Back in Manchester for a performance of *Invisible Cities* at the Mayfield Depot. After carving a story out of Italo Calvino's existential writing, knowing that projection and choreography needed to have a story to base themselves around, Lolita spent months not getting to see what those elements were while she was being asked, almost daily, to change her script in order to suit them. She is jumping through so many hoops while the importance of a good script is being underestimated.

Leo Warner is the visionary director who brought all the technical elements of dance and projection together. It looked amazing and was wonderful to watch, but at times I felt as though I was watching projection for projection's sake with the true idea linking every moment lost inside. Danny Sapani and Matthew Leonheart as Kublai Khan and Marco Polo respectively held the emotional line within the excellent movement and projections. Danny has incredible power and strong physical presence which is exactly what is needed to stand at the centre of this production. The wonderful choreography, performed by twenty-two of Rambert's stunning dancers, is jawdropping to watch. A brilliant technical achievement.

I can see Lolita slowly letting go of the responsibility she had to tell these stories. She is a little wasted after juggling her attendance at both rehearsals, while doing rewrites for each production. She sleeps on the long drive home.

Saturday 13 July

Adrian   It's 11.00 am and I'm at Mountview Theatre School in Peckham, about to teach a Taekwondo class, after which the senior grades will do a demonstration.

More students turn up to take part than I expected. It's nice of them and their parents to give up a Saturday in this way. Once the class is over, the demonstration begins and the senior grades jump and turn in the air, using various kicking techniques to break wooden boards. Finally I set up my thick polymer bricks, which I'm going to break with each hand but my mind keeps drifting off and thinking about work.

Sean Foley has agreed to put on *Calmer* at Birmingham Rep, with me directing. The timing seems good as Jasmine will have finished her GCSEs before Lolita and I begin work on it.

Cyrano has been announced in the West End with James McAvoy playing the lead (that was the person some of the theatres were talking about). Now I have the full picture, I can see why there was a lack of movement on our version. *Lottery Boy* hasn't got any money as yet, which leaves me and Luke very frustrated. We have been focused on this project for a while but have let our producer lead the charge. We are going to have to rethink our approach. The rights to the original book won't last forever and we may run out of time if we don't move quickly.

Back in the class, the bricks are set up for me to break. It's the last part of our demonstration. It's taken me years to learn how to break one of these with the back of my hand. I've been bruised, I've cut myself many times but I learned, in the end, that it's a mixture of conditioning and determination. The brick is an obstacle; you push your hand *through* it, not onto it. Some people go for a run or hit the gym to deal with their frustrations in life. I go to class.

I kneel down, take a moment to focus, then break the brick.

A few months later . . .

Adrian　We have just completed a three-day workshop on Lolita's play *Calmer* for Birmingham Rep. An invited audience of potential co-producers came to hear it. The response was positive. We'll have to wait and see what happens next.

Sean Foley asked me if I would be interested in being on the board of the Rep. It's a position I think will suit me very well. I can still remember performing in the studio there when I was fifteen and a member of Birmingham Youth Theatre.

The *Got It Covered* album that we recorded for Children In Need has sold more than 60,000 copies, raising just over £500,000 for the charity. Each of the artists involved was given a framed silver disc. That's one thing from my bucket list ticked off.

I recently had a meeting with Silva Screen Records about doing a solo album. There's a lot to work out and agree on, but I'm very excited by the prospect.

Life completed shooting in October 2019, and is now in the edit. We just had a photo shoot for the poster and other promotional material. It was nice to see the cast again and hear from the producers when it may be on television and how they will market the series next year.

I'm under a deadline to complete an essay on *Othello* in the next couple of weeks for Cambridge University Press. I've been trying to set aside the space in my head while meeting and taping for acting work that will start next year.

Lottery Boy has had some very good feedback from three producers both here and in the US. Although their appreciation of the writing has been good, turning that enthusiasm into any kind of solid commitment is a slow process. As people explain the funding and investment market, the uncertainty people feel regarding Britain's trade position, post Brexit, is clear. Although there is still nothing concrete, this new level of feedback on the script makes me very optimistic about next year.

But, as always, I have to wait and see what happens.

Lolita　*Life of Pi* is transferring to Wyndham's Theatre in London's West End in June 2020. It is then booked on a national tour and will also go to Canada. We have strong interest from North America and other countries. Max and I have been casting for London: the company will get bigger because we need understudies and alternates. We have been nominated for eleven national awards so far and won eight of them.

Invisible Cities played the Brisbane Festival in September 2019. I wasn't able to attend but heard that things ran smoothly and it was a more polished show. Next year[1] we will play in Kuwait and Hong Kong and I will have to adjust the script for a proscenium arch stage.

We've just done a workshop on *Calmer* for Birmingham Rep. It isn't officially announced yet but will go on next autumn.[2] Adrian is directing and I will be in it. I am so pleased and relieved that this play has found a home. It's been a long wait.

Hampstead Theatre are interested in *Politically Correct* and will have a reading of it in the New Year.[3] It'll be very useful to hear how it sounds in this ever-shifting political landscape.

I pitched *Testaments* to MIF AD John McGrath and he liked it but sadly we've just heard that they will not join us as co-producers. It was disappointing news but I will regroup with Marcus from the Roundhouse and the creative team to see where we go next.

I am in rehearsals with Kate Prince, artistic director of ZooNation, to dramaturg her new production for Sadler's Wells, *Message in a Bottle*. It opens next year[4] at the Peacock Theatre in London before going on tour. It's a dance piece and entirely Kate's story about refugees, but I am greatly enjoying helping her clarify the narrative within the amazing choreography and story she has so far.

As an actor, I have just finished filming for a new Amazon Prime series. I'm not allowed to say what it is, but it is an epic fantasy with a huge budget, an international cast and was shot in Prague and Slovenia. I play the mother of one of the leads.

Adrian and I recorded dramatic extracts for a new ten-part series for BBC Radio 4 called *Equal As We Are* about gender dynamics in literature and drama. We had fun reading ten scenes together, including Adam and Eve from Milton's *Paradise Lost*, Eliza Doolittle and Henry Higgins from George Bernard Shaw's *Pygmalion* and Hilary and Rupert from Jilly Cooper's *Riders*. Who said casting isn't opening up?

---

[1] 2020.

[2] 2020.

[3] Planned for March 2020, at the time of writing.

[4] Planned for February 2020, at the time of writing.

Next month, I am recording a new seven-part series called *This Thing of Darkness* for BBC Scotland for Radio 4. I am playing a forensic psychiatrist in a psychological thriller. It's a real page-turner.

And I have recently joined the board at Rambert and am very excited to be a part of their organization as they reinvent themselves. I have also joined the council at RADA and am equally pleased to be able to give back to the school that helped me do what I do.

And we have finished this diary!

I am very glad we did it. At the start it seemed like a big commitment but now I can see it has been good to mark how we work – the failures, the successes and everything in between. Adrian and I work hard to stay at the table. We throw so many balls in the air; some land and some don't. I suppose that's the requirement of the job – remain restless, never be complacent and always try.

ACKNOWLEDGEMENTS

We would like to thank:

Anna Brewer and her team at Methuen Drama for asking us to do this diary and guiding us along the way.

Tina Price, who read every draft, gave notes, and helped to realize the finished product. Her advice and friendship have been invaluable.

Our agents – Sue Latimer at ARG, Sarah MacCormick at Curtis Brown and Katie Haines at The Agency – who helped us get the opportunities for the work detailed in this diary. Their guidance and support have made our careers what they are.

And finally, Dr Oliver Neville who was principal of RADA when we auditioned and whose decision it was to let us both in! We're very grateful to that place, it's where we met. Without Oliver's passionate leadership we wouldn't have got the training we had, and the career prospects it provided.

INDEX